THE
TIME
MANAGEMENT
WORKSHOP

THE
TIME
MANAGEMENT
WORKSHOP

A Trainer's Guide

Patricia Haddock

AMACOM
American Management Association
New York • Atlanta • Boston • Chicago • Kansas City • San Francisco • Washington, D. C.
Brussels • Mexico City • Tokyo • Toronto

Special discounts on bulk quantities of AMACOM books are
available to corporations, professional associations, and other
organizations. For details, contact Special Sales Department,
AMACOM, a division of American Management Association,
1601 Broadway, New York, NY 10019.
Tel.: 212-903-8316. Fax: 212-903-8083.
Web site: www.amacombooks.org

This publication is designed to provide accurate and authoritative
information in regard to the subject matter covered. It is sold with
the understanding that the publisher is not engaged in rendering
legal, accounting, or other professional service. If legal advice or
other expert assistance is required, the services of a competent
professional person should be sought.

Library of Congress Cataloging-in-Publication Data

Haddock, Patricia.
    The time management workshop : a trainer's guide / Patricia Haddock.
        p. cm.
    Includes index.
    ISBN 0-8144-7082-3
    1. Time management—Study and teaching—Handbooks, manuals, etc.
  2. Employees—Training of—Handbooks, manuals, etc. I. Title.

HD69.T54 H343 2000
658.3'1244—dc21

                                                00-055829

Printing number

10 9 8 7 6 5 4 3 2 1

CONTENTS

PART III: DAY TWO   127

THE
TIME
MANAGEMENT
WORKSHOP

Agenda

Day One

8:00–8:30	Administrative Details (30 minutes)
8:30–10:00	Module 1: Time Management vs. Productivity (1.5 hours)
10:00–10:15	Break
10:15–12:15	Module 2: Getting Organized (2 hours)
12:15–1:15	Lunch
1:15–2:45	Module 3: Developing Concentration and Focus (1.5 hours)
2:45–3:00	Break
3:00–5:00	Module 4: Making Friends with Procrastination (2 hours)

Day Two

8:00–8:25	Review Day One (25 minutes)
8:30–10:00	Module 5: Understanding Work Styles (1.5 hours)
10:00–10:15	Break
10:15–11:45	Module 6: Mastering Meetings (1.5 hours)
11:45–12:30	Lunch
12:30–1:30	Module 7: Decision Making and Setting Priorities (1 hour)
1:30–1:45	Break
1:45–3:45	Module 8: Creating Balance and Setting Boundaries (2 hours)
3:45–4:00	Break
4:00–5:00	Module 9: Managing Time on the Road and Course Assessment (1 hour)

PART I

BACKGROUND AND PREPARATION

This book gives you everything you need to facilitate a two-day time management workshop. It is organized in nine modules, which can be delivered as stand-alone workshops or combined in any way that meets your needs. It can be used by both new and experienced trainers.

The workshop is designed to help facilitate learning and transfer knowledge and skills to participants. To this end, it relies on participant interaction and involvement. Each module includes the following:

- Objectives
- Agenda
- Commentary
- Individual Exercises
- Team Activities
- Group Discussions

USING THIS BOOK FOR MAXIMUM RESULTS

To achieve maximum results with this book, you should do the following:

1. Read Part I, which gives you general information about the workshop and explains how to use the book and plan, prepare for, and deliver the workshop with confidence, as well as hone your presentation skills so that participants' needs are met.

2. Review the Table of Contents and Agenda for an overview of the modules covered by the book.

3. Become familiar with Parts II and III, the contents of the workshop, with Part II representing Day One and Part III representing Day Two.

- Commentary gives you information about the topic in order to deliver the workshop. Please study this material thoroughly. The more familiar you are with this information, the easier it will be to facilitate the program since it is important that you deliver each module without reading the Commentary verbatim.

- Handouts support the information in the Commentary sections and allow participants to relate the information to their environment. Handouts are valuable job aids that can be referred to after the workshop ends. Distribute handouts during the workshop at designated times, not at the beginning of the workshop. You can copy the handouts directly from the book or customize them with your company logo. Make sure you complete the handouts with your own responses before delivering the workshop. This will help you understand how they work so you can anticipate questions from participants.

- Overheads can be directly copied onto transparencies, although it is recommended that you add clip art to enliven learning.

- Notes are to be given to participants at the beginning of the workshop. They can be used by participants for personal note taking.

4. Study Module 6: Mastering Meetings and do the exercises found there. This module contains valuable information to help you facilitate the workshop.

YOUR ROLE AS A TRAINER

As the trainer, the success of the workshop will be determined by your ability to engage participants in the learning process and to transfer skills and knowledge to them. This part of the book will help you prepare for your role as trainer.

Your primary goal is to teach participants new skills that improve their productivity and efficiency. In order to do this, you need to engage participants and show them how the information in the workshop applies to their jobs. Participants expect you to be a subject matter expert and will look to you to help them make connections between theory and practice.

Familiarity with the information in each module is key to a successful workshop. The more time you spend learning the material, the more confident you will feel and the more confidence you will communicate.

Adults learn best in interactive programs where they can participate in the learning process. The design of the workshop helps you do this by intermingling group discussions, individual exercises, and team activities.

One of your responsibilities is to create an atmosphere where participants feel safe interacting with each other and practicing new behaviors. You want to encourage audience participation and provide guidance for exercises and activities. This requires you to understand both group and individual behavior so you can control the workshop without taking over.

Another important responsibility is to ensure that each module begins and ends on time. You need to monitor group discussions and keep team activities and individual exercises on track and on time. You must be able to identify and concentrate on key points and know which activities can be skipped or abbreviated if you are behind schedule, or extended if you are ahead of schedule.

One of the most important ways of ensuring a successful workshop is to customize it for your audience.

CUSTOMIZING THE WORKSHOP

While the workshop modules can be delivered as is, it is better to customize them so that participants can understand how the concepts relate to their jobs and how the strategies can be applied to what they do. Customization is not difficult and can be accomplished in a number of ways:

- One of the most important tools for customizing the workshop is to perform a needs assessment to determine what you want the workshop to accomplish. You can conduct a needs assessment by asking participants and/or managers to complete a questionnaire, or you can conduct focus groups or one-on-one interviews to identify the problems and challenges that will be addressed through training.

  A needs assessment may also reveal factors that cannot be resolved through training. For example, if low morale is contributing to decreased productivity, you may need more than a time management workshop to increase productivity. For example, you may discover that employees would benefit from stress management or conflict resolution workshops. Perhaps managers need training in coaching. As the trainer, you want to focus on problems and challenges that can be positively impacted through this workshop, not on problems and challenges that need to be addressed in other ways.

- After you have conducted your needs assessment, set goals for the workshop and define the measures you will use to determine the success of the workshop. Measurements should be quantifiable—an increase in customer calls, an increase in sales closed, etc. Establishing clear outcomes determines what you will emphasize and how you will structure the workshop. Identify the skills and knowledge you want participants to learn and acquire from the workshop, and describe any new behaviors you want them to demonstrate on the job.

- Understand the makeup of your audience—participants' ages, gender, cultural background, education, position, etc.—so you can better tailor examples and exercises and create relevance for them.

- Determine how well participants know each other since this can affect group dynamics, rapport, and willingness to participate.
- Determine how much participants already know about the topic.
- Determine which modules participants need and their order of delivery.
- Decide what format works best for participants:
  - *Continuous format:* The entire workshop is delivered in two days.
  - *Spaced format:* The modules are delivered discontinuously over a period of time. For example, you may decide to deliver one module every Monday until all the modules are delivered. Some things to consider in determining format are business needs, staffing requirements, the need for phone coverage, customer service demands, and work flow.
- Identify any subject matter experts in the audience. You may want to acknowledge their expertise and ask them to contribute actively to the workshop. Sometimes, subject matter experts "take over" the workshop. You can control this by working with them before the workshop to clarify what you want them to contribute and how.
- Add examples from your organization or replace the examples in the Commentary sections with ones that are more reflective of your business or industry. The more pertinent you make the examples, the easier it will be for participants to apply the information to their situation.
- Incorporate any relevant news about your company or industry. Identify corporate themes that can be integrated into the program, such as the corporate vision, values, and mission. Find out what's happening in the departments where participants work.
- Decide if you will need visuals for empty wall spaces and, if so, develop them. For example, you may want to post entertaining quotes about time management or your company's vision and mission statements. Copy the text onto flipchart pages and place them around the room.
- Decide if you will distribute novelty items or rewards for participants and teams who answer questions or successfully complete activities. For example, you may want to give out items like coffee cups or pens with your company logo.
- Prepare certificates of completion using your company logo, and send them to participants who complete the two-day program.

PREPARING FOR THE WORKSHOP

If attendance at the workshop is voluntary, announce the workshop about four weeks before it is scheduled. Publicize it using the company newsletter, memos, emails, voicemails, personal phone calls, announcements at meetings, etc.

Determine how many people you want in each session. Keep the number of participants under twenty, if possible. The more people in attendance, the more time is needed to complete exercises and maintain order. If necessary, schedule more than one session. Determine any special needs or disability accommodations that may be required.

Have a backup plan. What will you do if the overhead projector dies? The microphone stops working? Only three people show up when twelve were expected? Or forty people arrive and you were expecting only ten? Have a plan for anything that may go wrong.

Study the Commentary for each module, and do the exercises and activities. Create talking points on 3- by 5-inch cards (your "talking points" cards) to ensure that you cover the most important information in each module. Make sure your cards are easy to read and serve as memory triggers so that you can use them as memory aids when you rehearse and deliver the workshop.

Identify which group discussions, team activities, and individual exercises can be skipped if time runs short. Note that Module 1: Time Management and Productivity contains exercises that are fundamental to the entire program and should always be delivered in its entirety.

In addition, as stated previously, you should review Module 6: Mastering Meetings and follow the information contained there about preparing for the meeting.

Use the Workshop Checklist that appears later in this section to ensure that you have everything you need to present a professional workshop.

Enlivening the Presentation and Making the Event Memorable

Customization is one of the best ways to make your workshop memorable. The more relevant you make it, the more people will remember it positively.

Humor can enliven your presentation and help people remember information. However, if used inappropriately, humor can alienate your entire audience. Never use off-color or racist jokes or tell stories that perpetuate stereotypes. Don't insert "funny" lines in your material. Leave the one-liners to stand-up comics.

By contrast, one of the best ways to add humor is with storytelling. Stories are also a wonderful way to enliven a presentation. Personal anecdotes are best. Look at your own life to find experiences that are relevant to the subject and that participants can relate to.

Using your own foibles, mistakes, and successes as examples also draws you closer to participants and helps establish rapport with them. People will recognize themselves in your stories, and you can get your points across without being didactic. For example, if you want participants to share stories about procrastination, you can begin by sharing a story about your own procrastination style. Remember, though, that while making gentle fun of yourself is fine, you should never demean anyone else.

If you use stories from sources other than your life, make sure you credit the source. For example, if you use a story or anecdote from *Inc.*, make sure you tell the audience where it came from. Keep in mind that you cannot use stories originated by professional speakers, even if you give them credit.

Practice telling your stories before the session so you feel comfortable with them.

Rehearsing the Workshop

No matter how well you know the material, you need to rehearse what you are going to say and how you are going to work with the handouts and overheads. Rehearsing helps you learn the material so that you become comfortable with it. This can help you handle any nervousness you may feel about presenting. The more you rehearse, the smoother your delivery will become. But don't try to be perfect. If you try for perfection, you will most likely appear stilted and overly formal. You want to appear human and approachable.

While reading the Commentary verbatim is not acceptable and can actually impede learning, referring to your talking points cards is fine. After you have delivered the workshop a few times, you will no longer need your talking points cards since the information will be so familiar to you.

Using your talking points cards, tape yourself giving the presentation, and listen to the tape to evaluate factors such as timing, word emphasis, and ease in communicating important points. Watching your timing is very important since the workshop covers a lot of material in two days, and your pace should not be too fast or too slow.

Look for fillers such as "um" and "er" or phrases such as "you know" or "right." If you discover that you use such syllables or phrases, pay closer attention to your speech patterns and learn to pause instead of using fillers.

Practice handling the overheads smoothly and become familiar with what is on each one. You should not read the overhead by looking at it. Instead, keep your attention on participants as you show the overhead. This means that you have to either memorize the text on each overhead or create a 3- by 5-inch talking points card for it. When you put up an overhead, allow about five seconds of silence for people to process it. If you point to something on the overhead, use a pencil, pen, or pointer—not your finger. Avoid using laser pointers. They can be hard to follow, and many people don't like them.

Handouts should be distributed when you are instructed to do so. In some cases, you do not want participants reading handouts or doing exercises before you deliver the prerequisite Commentary information. Practice distributing the handouts and explaining what you want participants to do and/or accomplish for each activity and exercise. Anticipate questions and develop answers.

If you are unfamiliar with using a microphone and the size of the room or number of participants requires the use of one, find out what kind of mike you will be using, learn how it works, and practice using it.

Visualize a successful presentation. Run a movie in your mind, adding details and practicing your comments. Make sure your mental movie is positive and upbeat.

Putting Together a First-Aid Kit

Every trainer needs a "first-aid kit" of items that may be needed during the presentation. You cannot rely on having any of these items available unless you bring them with you.

✓ First-Aid Kit Checklist

❏ AA and AAA batteries
❏ Blank name tags
❏ Blank 3- by 5-inch cards
❏ Blank transparencies
❏ Bottled water to make sure you can hydrate your throat during the presentation
❏ Calendar
❏ Clock
❏ Colored adhesive dots
❏ Duplicate copies of overheads
❏ Extra pantyhose (for women trainers)
❏ Extra tampons or feminine napkins (for women trainers)
❏ Flipchart markers
❏ Masking tape
❏ Master handouts
❏ Nail file
❏ Nonprescription pain remedies
❏ Paper clips
❏ Paper towels
❏ Pencils and pens
❏ Pointer
❏ Post-it® Notes
❏ Scissors
❏ Scotch tape
❏ Stapler and staples
❏ Tacks or pushpins
❏ Tent cards
❏ Throat lozenges
❏ Tissues
❏ Unlined and lined paper
❏ Whiteboard markers and eraser

DELIVERING THE WORKSHOP
Before the Workshop Begins
✓ The Day before the Workshop

❑ Make sure your handouts have been copied and are collated for easy distribution.

❑ Double-check overheads and put them in sequence.

❑ Make sure you have everything in your "first-aid kit."

❑ Confirm the workshop site and time.

❑ Get directions to the workshop site, if necessary, and plan your route if you are driving. Allow time for traffic and getting lost!

❑ Place colored dots on name tags to facilitate the formation of triads. On Day One, you will organize participants into triads based on the colored dots on their name tags.

❑ Eat a light dinner and get a good night's sleep.

✓ The Day of the Workshop

❑ Arrive at the workshop location at least thirty minutes before the workshop is scheduled to begin.

❑ Go over the items on your Workshop Checklist and make sure you have everything you need.

❑ Make sure the room is set up as you directed. If not, arrange for it to be corrected before participants arrive.

❑ Test all electronic equipment.

❑ Place the overhead screen and flipchart so all participants can see them. Flipchart tripods (easels) should be steady, and markers should have ink in them.

❑ Focus the overhead projector.

❑ Make sure that you have enough handouts for all the participants and that they are ready to be distributed as needed.

❑ Correct any environmental problems, such as temperatures that are too warm or too cold, noise from external sources, and bad lighting.

❑ Make sure your overheads are in the right sequence for delivery.

❑ Test the microphone if you are going to use one, and learn how to turn it on and off.

  • If you are using a handheld mike, learn how to remove it from the stand, and practice moving around with it, especially if it has a cord.
  • If you are using a lapel mike, clip the battery pack to your belt or slip it into a pocket. Place the mike on your lapel a few inches below chin level.

WORKSHOP CHECKLIST

Instructor:

Title of program:

Date: Time:

Location:

Number of participants:

Location of facilities, i.e., cafeteria, coffee shop, bathrooms, etc.:

Room arrangement: ___ classroom ___ auditorium ___ U-shaped

Check the following materials as needed:

	Need	Obtained
Meeting room	_____	_____
Tables and chairs		
Quantities: Tables	_____	_____
Chairs	_____	_____
Breakout rooms	_____	_____
Tables for supplies/materials/etc.	_____	_____
Overhead projector and screen	_____	_____
Overhead transparencies	_____	_____
LCD projector and screen	_____	_____
Computer	_____	_____
Flipchart and markers	_____	_____
Whiteboard and markers	_____	_____
Slide projector	_____	_____
Video equipment	_____	_____
Audio equipment	_____	_____

	Need	Obtained
Handheld microphone	_____	_____
Lapel microphone	_____	_____
A/V technical support	_____	_____
Water and glasses	_____	_____
Refreshments	_____	_____
Coffee	_____	_____
Tea	_____	_____
Soft drinks	_____	_____
Juice	_____	_____
Breakfast	_____	_____
Lunch	_____	_____
Snacks	_____	_____
Handouts	_____	_____
Masking tape	_____	_____
Writing materials	_____	_____
Paper	_____	_____
Pens	_____	_____
Notepads/unlined paper	_____	_____
Tent card/name tags	_____	_____

PARTICIPANT ROSTER

Instructor:

Title of Program:

Date: Time:

Location:

Participant Name	Department	Phone Number	Email Address

- Ask someone to stand in the back of the room and listen while you adjust the volume on the microphone.
- Remember to turn off a handheld mike before setting it down on a table and turn off a lapel mike before and during every break.

❑ Welcome participants as they arrive, and ask them to sign the Participant Roster. Chat with people. Find out what they do. Be accessible and friendly.

Getting Off to a Good Start

Start on time. Don't make prompt people wait for people who are tardy.

Realize that many adults come to workshops with memories of bad experiences from school. Thus, you want to make them feel comfortable quickly. Explain how the workshop will work, and clearly state what you expect. Review the agenda and explain how to use the Notes and Handouts. If you are training coworkers, put them at ease, especially if you have a management job and they don't. A good way to do this is to describe your role in the company and any jobs you may hold that are similar to theirs. Otherwise they may feel intimidated by your position with the company.

You may have to overcome resistance and reluctance from the audience, especially if attendance at the workshop is mandatory. If that is the case, acknowledge that participants have not had a choice about attendance, and emphasize the benefits the workshop offers. Explain how the information in the workshop applies to them and how they will be able to use it both on and off the job to make things easier. Give them good reasons for actively participating, and make them eager to learn by emphasizing what the workshop offers.

Don't talk down to participants. Show patience if some participants are slow learners. Always treat everyone with respect.

Handling Nerves

About 80 percent of the population suffers from stage fright, and you may as well. For some people, speaking is more frightening than the prospect of dying! It will be easier for you if you think of yourself as a teacher rather than a public speaker. Just be yourself. Participants may be more nervous than you are since they don't know what to expect. You, in turn, control the room and the workshop.

Before people begin arriving, find a private place to warm up. Shake your body out and do shoulder and neck rolls to relax your muscles. Make "lion" faces to relax your facial muscles. You do this by opening your mouth wide as if you were a lion ready to roar. You can also make exaggerated chewing movements to loosen your jaw. Before you begin speaking, take several deep "belly" breaths to fill your lungs with oxygen. Imagine that you are anchored to the earth by a large network of roots, like a tree.

Have water handy to lubricate your mouth if it gets dry. Skip the ice since it will constrict your vocal cords. Avoid caffeinated drinks, which can aggravate nerves, and milk products, which can produce excessive mucus.

Stop worrying about how well you will perform. Participants don't expect perfection. They want you to appear confident and competent. The more you think about your performance, the more nervous you will feel. Instead, concentrate on the participants and how the information you will be giving them can make their lives easier. Remember: One of your responsibilities as a trainer is to make participants feel comfortable.

Understanding How to Deliver Information

People have very short attention spans. You need to grab their attention and keep it, or they will turn you off just as they turn off a television program that bores them. How do you keep their interest?

Not by delivering a speech but by having a conversation. Start by using language that appeals to all the dominant senses: sight, hearing, and touch. This is a good way of establishing rapport and ensuring that participants understand the information. In addition, everyone has a favorite way of thinking: visual, auditory, or kinesthetic. By using language that appeals to all three, you will address everyone in your audience. The following table gives words and phrases to help you do this.

Words and Phrases That Appeal to Visual, Auditory, and Kinesthetic Ways of Thinking

Visual	Auditory	Kinesthetic
Look	Say	Touch
Picture	Ring	Push
Imagine	Ask	Rub
Reflect	Clear	Solid
Clarify	Discuss	Rough
Focus	Listen	Tackle
Outlook	Tell	Tension
See	Quiet	Temperature
I see what you mean	On the same wavelength	I'll keep in touch
Let's look at this	Tell me about it	I feel it in my gut
Let me show you what I mean	Let me tell you what I mean	I feel that it should be this way
Shed some light on the subject	Music to my ears	Going to pieces
It appears to me	In a manner of speaking	Put my finger on it
To illustrate	It's all Greek to me	I can't grasp that
The future looks dim	That sounds bad	Rubs me the wrong way

Ask questions throughout the workshop to determine whether participants are learning the material. Address questions to the entire group, rather than singling out one person, and clearly phrase questions so that participants know what you want. A good question to evaluate learning is to ask participants how they will apply information when they return to the office or what they will do differently as a result of the training. Allow enough time for responses, and give credit for all answers. There are no wrong answers!

Encourage people to ask questions. Questions from the audience can tell you if people are absorbing the material or if they are confused. Always repeat the question to make sure you understand it.

If people seem confused, slow down and ask more questions as you go along to make sure people are keeping up with you. On the other hand, if people seem bored, pick up the pace and move things along more quickly.

If someone asks a question you know will be answered later, tell him you will be getting to it. If it is inconvenient to answer the question when it is asked, have him write it down so you can be sure to address it later. You don't want to disrupt the flow of the workshop. But of course, you want to make participants feel like their questions are welcome.

If you are asked a question of fact and you don't know the answer, don't get defensive and don't bluff an answer. Admit you don't know the answer, and ask if anyone in the room can answer it. Open the floor to participation and ask for input. If a satisfactory answer doesn't come forth, tell the person who asked the question that you will research it during a break. If you need more time to find the answer, tell her you will get back to her after the workshop. Make sure you take her phone number or email address and send an answer as soon as you return to your office and can research it.

If you are asked for your opinion and you don't have an immediate response, give yourself time to think about the answer and collect your thoughts. Ask the participant if you can get back to him after you have considered it, and make sure to return to the question when you are ready to answer it.

If you notice that people seem restless, take an unscheduled energizer. Do a five-minute "share" where each participant talks to five people for one minute each and tells them one success story related to the topic, or ask them to share one action item they intend to implement.

Maintaining a high energy level is necessary especially if you do the full two-day workshop. Both your energy and that of the participants will ebb and flow during the program. (See Module 5: Understanding Work Styles for information on activity cycles.) You need to plan for the ebb times when energy is low. A good way to pick up energy is to get people moving. Have them stand and stretch or do some marching in place. Don't have them rub someone else's shoulders or touch another person.

Candy, energy bars, and fruit can be effective energizers. Just make sure you tell people what contains sugar and what doesn't, since some people don't or can't eat sugar.

Walk around the room and increase your own energy level. This will focus attention on you and raise the energy level of the room.

Breaks are an important part of the workshop. They help keep people alert and provide an opportunity for them to get to know each other better. Breaks also contribute to recall of information. Experiments have shown that a ten-minute break every hour improves memory. Breaks also give people a chance to move around and exercise their bodies. Call a stretch break if participants seem restless, bored, or listless.

Delivery Dos and Don'ts

Dos

- Use a conversational tone.
- Move around purposefully every few minutes.
- Use a variety of hand and facial gestures.
- Smile at participants and use their first names.
- Stand still when delivering important points or instructions.
- Move toward the audience for emphasis.
- Change your voice inflection to add variety and interest.
- Speak loudly enough to be heard at the back of the room. Use a microphone if you are speaking to more than twenty-five people.
- Maintain an erect posture.
- Use first and second person when you speak.
- Use action verbs and inclusive language.
- Use good diction and correct pronunciation.
- Use pauses to create emphasis and get people's attention.
- Speak with a moderate pace.
- Make eye contact with people in every part of the room.
- Pick up your pace after lunch when people tend to get sleepy.

Don'ts

- Preach to the room.
- Use slang, jargon, or clichés.
- Stand behind a lectern or table.
- Use only masculine pronouns.
- Sway back and forth or bounce up and down.
- Use passive voice.
- Correct people.
- Argue with participants.
- Go off on tangents.
- Block the overhead screen.

- Pace nervously.
- Tell jokes.
- Look at only one or two people.

Understanding Group Dynamics and Controlling the Room

Groups have distinctive personalities. Some groups are lively and expressive, with participants eagerly contributing. Other groups are quiet and reserved, and participants must be drawn out.

Generally, the group will take on a life of its own and things will move along smoothly. However, sometimes things go wrong. For example, someone may begin to monopolize discussions, an exercise or activity may not work the way it should, or participants may become confused. If this happens, stop and take action. Take a short break if you can't decide what to do. When you reconvene, immediately take charge and implement your decision. (See Module 6: Mastering Meetings for more information on how to handle conflicts and difficult people.)

Facilitating Exercises and Encouraging Participation

This workshop uses group discussions, team activities, and individual exercises to facilitate learning and encourage participation. When using all of these, make sure you watch the clock and stay on schedule.

Group discussions.   Each module has several group discussions. These are structured opportunities for participants to become involved in the program, interpret information, and share experiences and opinions. Most discussions will include key points. Don't just give the key points to participants; lead the discussion so that these points are delivered by participants. Motivate participation by giving positive feedback and encouraging responses. You may want to give prizes, such as logo items or candy, as rewards for participating.

Team activities and individual exercises.   Each module has several team activities, to be done by participants broken up into small groups. People who are reluctant to speak in a large group may be more comfortable in a smaller group. Team activities are designed to encourage interaction among members of the team and help them apply what they are learning to their particular situations.

Individual exercises are designed to be done privately. Often, the subject of the exercise is highly personal or requires the participants to reveal information they may not want someone else to know. The questions they answer in individual exercises require introspection and quiet time.

For each activity and exercise, distribute the handout and show the appropriate overhead. Clearly give instructions for each activity and exercise and explain what you want them to accomplish. Use the Commentary for this. Always ask for questions.

Walk around the room during the exercise or activity. Be available for questions that arise while people are working. If the whole group will benefit from the answer, repeat the question and answer for the entire class.

During group activities, observe how members are working together. If one person seems to be dominating a team, you may want to intervene and make sure everyone has a chance to participate. You can do this by moving into the team, listening for a while, then using questions to involve other team members.

After the exercise, debrief by asking participants or teams to share the results of their activity or exercise. Rely on volunteers for this. Don't force people to participate or embarrass someone for not wanting to share.

AFTER THE WORKSHOP

Many workshops end with a whimper instead of a bang. How well you end the workshop affects people's evaluation of its effectiveness. A good way to end is with a personal story that summarizes one or more main points from the workshop. Then distribute "Certificates of Achievement" to all participants. Always allow enough time for participants to complete the formal evaluation before leaving the room.

Using Evaluations to Improve

There are two types of evaluations to be performed after the workshop: (1) evaluations by participants on the effectiveness of the workshop and your facilitation skills, and (2) effectiveness evaluation—your evaluation of how well the workshop met the goals you set for it.

Participant evaluations. Asking people to evaluate the workshop is a humbling exercise. You want them to evaluate both the content and your delivery. See the Course Assessment handout at the end of this section.

Review all evaluations for ideas on how to improve the workshop and your performance. Keep in mind that your goal is to give participants something of value. Most of the time, you will succeed, but as the saying goes, you can't please all the people all the time.

Effectiveness evaluation. This is your opportunity to evaluate if the workshop met the objectives you set for it. Review the objectives you determined before the workshop began. Did employees become more productive as a result of the workshop?

Wait two weeks to one month after the end of the workshop to evaluate its effectiveness. Review the measures you established and compare them to employees' performance. Were the measures met? If not, determine why. Can the workshop be changed to make it more effective?

You can interview participants and their supervisors or peers either one-on-one or in focus groups to obtain anecdotal evaluations of the workshop and how applicable the information is once people are back on the job. You can also use the same questionnaire you used for the needs assessment to discover how responses have changed.

CERTIFICATE OF ACHIEVEMENT

Instructor:

Title of program:

Date:

Location:

This certifies that _____ [name] has successfully completed the Time Management Workshop on _____ [date].

[Instructor's signature]

COURSE ASSESSMENT

Instructor:

Title of Program:

Date: Time:

Location:

For each item below, check the box that corresponds to the number that you believe applies to the item.

  1 = Strongly disagree
  2 = Disagree
  3 = Not sure
  4 = Agree
  5 = Strongly agree

Item	1	2	3	4	5
I can apply the information from the workshop on my job.					
I can relate to the examples and problems in the workshop.					
I learned new skills to use on the job.					
I would recommend this workshop to other employees.					
Information was clearly communicated.					
Learning objectives for the workshop were clear.					
Learning objectives for the workshop were met.					
The handouts made it easier to apply the information to my job.					
The handouts were easy to use.					
The instructor was organized and efficient.					
The instructor encouraged participation.					
The instructor handled group discussions well.					
The instructor handled questions well.					
The instructor kept my interest.					

Item	1	2	3	4	5
The instructor knew the material.					
The instructor maintained control of the class.					
The instructor used examples I could relate to.					
The instructor used overheads effectively.					
The instructor was well prepared.					
The instructor's delivery was lively and interesting.					
The length of the workshop was about right.					
The modules were presented in a logical manner.					
The overheads added to the presentation.					
The overheads made it easier to understand the material.					
The pace of the workshop was appropriate.					
The individual exercises helped me apply the information to my job.					
The room was comfortable.					
The team activities were valuable.					
The workshop was fun.					

I believe that the workshop could be improved in the following way(s):

I liked these aspects of the workshop:

PART II

DAY ONE

Administrative Details, Time Management, and Productivity

ADMINISTRATIVE DETAILS (30 MINUTES)
OBJECTIVES

- Establish your expertise for teaching this class.
- Provide an overview of the program.
- Introduce participants to each other.
- Review program objectives.
- Review safety information.

MATERIALS NEEDED

- Overhead 0.1: Welcome to Time Management
- Overhead 0.2: Program Objectives
- Overhead 0.3: Program Objectives (continued)

AGENDA

Welcome Participants and Review Administrative Details	5 minutes
Review Program Objectives	5 minutes
Describe Program Norms	5 minutes
Set Up Work Teams	15 minutes

WELCOME PARTICIPANTS AND REVIEW ADMINISTRATIVE DETAILS (5 MINUTES)

 Show Overhead 0.1: Welcome to Time Management.

Welcome to Time Management
0.1   © 2001 Patricia Haddock.

Facilitator: Call the room to order. Ask participants to take their seats so the program can begin. Introduce yourself and describe your role and expertise. Explain how the program will be conducted.

Commentary

- The program will run for two days.
- Each day will start promptly at [time]. Encourage people to arrive on time.
- You will provide breaks throughout each day so they can use the restroom, retrieve messages, return calls, and get to know each other better.
- Go over safety information, i.e., location of exits, etc.
- Provide location of restrooms, coffee rooms, etc.

Ask for questions.

REVIEW PROGRAM OBJECTIVES (5 MINUTES)

Question: How many minutes are there in a twenty-four–hour day?

Answer: Encourage responses until you get the right answer: 1,440 minutes.

Commentary

You have 1,440 minutes in a twenty-four–hour day. You spend about 480 of those minutes sleeping. You devote the remaining 960 minutes to living and making a living. Some people get a lot done and seem to squeeze more out of their day. Others spend their time running around looking busy, but not getting things done. Checking items off a to-do list is less important than doing the right things. You need to produce results. You do this not by managing time but by managing yourself.

Think of time in the same way you think of money. You probably don't have all your money in a savings account that pays only a small amount of interest. It makes financial sense to invest your money for the best possible return. This same principle applies to time. You want to invest your time in activities that produce the greatest returns.

Do you spend your time wisely and invest it in activities that produce results? Do you know what things should be dropped or delegated? Do you understand what's important, and are you doing it? Do you make things easier for yourself, or harder?

 Show Overhead 0.2: Program Objectives.

> **Program Objectives**
>
> - Discover where your time goes.
> - Reduce time wasters.
> - Get organized.
> - Build on your strengths.
> - Work with others.
>
> 0.2

Over the next two days, you will:

- Discover where your time goes in order to ensure that you are investing it in activities that contribute most to your productivity.

- Reduce time-wasting activities, interruptions, and distractions.

- Get and stay organized.

- Build on your personal strengths.

- Work more effectively with others in order to get things done.

 Show Overhead 0.3: Program Objectives (continued).

> **Program Objectives (continued)**
>
> - Develop focus.
> - Make decisions and prioritize activities.
> - Manage meetings.
> - Make friends with procrastination.
> - Create balance.
>
> 0.3

- Develop concentration and focus.

- Make decisions and set priorities.

- Spend less time at meetings.

- Make friends with procrastination and use it to become more productive.

- Create balance.

Ask for questions.

DESCRIBE PROGRAM NORMS (5 MINUTES)

Commentary

This program is highly interactive, and it is important that everyone participates. Much of its value will come from the sharing of information among you.

In order to encourage participation, please raise your hand before speaking so that we avoid speaking over the top of each other.

There are no right or wrong answers. This program is very pragmatic. What works for one person may not work for another—or it may be the solution to your problem. Everyone's opinion counts.

In your handouts, you will receive a set of pages called "Notes," one for each module. As we go through the workshop, you can use these pages to take notes and write down information you want to remember so you can refer to it after the workshop ends. The more thorough your notes, the more valuable they will be later when you need to refer to them.

Ask for questions.

SET UP WORK TEAMS (15 MINUTES)
Commentary

Many of the exercises are designed to be done in small groups. We are going to form teams of three people who will work together throughout the next two days. It's best to work with people who don't know you and don't have any preconceived ideas about your work styles or work habits.

When you arrived, you received a name tag with a colored dot on it. There are three colors: blue, green, and yellow. We are going to form teams so that one of each color is represented in each team.

For example, here are three people, each of whom has a different colored dot on their name tags. We will form them into a team. Any questions? Form your teams now.

 Facilitator: Select three people at random, each of whom has a different colored dot, and form them into a team as an example. Allow time for the teams to form; then call the room to order.

Choose one member of the team to be the record taker or record keeper. This person will record the results of each team activity and report the results to the rest of the class. Choose your record keeper now.

 Facilitator: Ask that all record keepers raise their hands. Ask if any record keeper needs paper, and if so, pass out tablets.

Now, choose another member of your team to be the timekeeper. This person will make sure that everyone has a turn during team activities and that your team stays on schedule. Choose your timekeeper now.

 Facilitator: Ask that all timekeepers raise their hands.

Team Activity: Team Introductions

Instructions to Participants: It's important that you get to know the people in your team. We're going to take ten minutes for you to get to know each other. Take turns, introduce yourself, explain your job, and tell what time management problems you hope to solve by the end of the workshop. The record keeper will list these problems for the team.

Ask for questions.

 Facilitator: Bring the room to order.

Debriefing: Call on three to five teams to describe the time management problems they identified. Write them on the flipchart and post the pages around the room along with several blank flipchart pages.

Sometime between now and the end of the day, will each record keeper take a few minutes to write the time management problems your team identified on the posted flipchart pages? That way we'll be sure to address everyone's issues by the end of the program tomorrow.

Ask for questions.

Time Management
vs. Productivity
(1.5 Hours)

OBJECTIVES FOR MODULE 1

- Understand the difference between time management and productivity.
- Identify how participants currently spend time.
- Identify time wasters and create strategies for eliminating them.
- Set goals.
- Understand how planning improves productivity.

MATERIALS NEEDED

- Handout 1.1: Sample Time Log
- Handout 1.2: Time Log
- Handout 1.3: Identifying Time Wasters
- Handout 1.4: Doing What's Most Important
- Handout 1.5: Set SMART Goals
- Handout 1.6: Sample Set SMART Goals
- Handout 1.7: Planning to Reach Your Goals
- Overhead 1.1: Time Management vs. Productivity

- Overhead 1.2: Objectives for Module 1
- Overhead 1.3: The Value of Goals
- Overhead 1.4: SMART Goals
- Overhead 1.5: The Benefits of Planning

AGENDA

Time Management vs. Productivity	5 minutes
Objectives for Module 1	5 minutes
Where Does Your Time Go?	10 minutes
Identifying Time Wasters	20 minutes
Identifying and Setting Goals	30 minutes
Planning to Improve Productivity	20 minutes

TIME MANAGEMENT VS. PRODUCTIVITY (5 MINUTES)

Show Overhead 1.1: Time Management vs. Productivity.

> *Time Management vs. Productivity*
>
> 1.1   © 2001 Patricia Haddock

Commentary

How many people have taken a class or workshop on time management? Raise your hands.

How many have read a book on time management?

How many have listened to a tape?

You don't have to raise your hand for this question. How many people left the time management class they took, closed the book or turned off the tape, implemented the suggestions for about a week or maybe a month, then slipped back into the habits that led you to the time management material in the first place?

Most people find themselves back where they started not long after taking a class, reading a book, or listening to a time management tape.

Why does this happen? Why don't time management strategies work? Ask for answers from participants.

Traditional techniques usually offer a leftbrain, logical, linear approach to getting things done. They emphasize creating and maintaining order and *controlling* time. Time, however, cannot be controlled. Time flows, and in order to become more productive, you have to learn how to flow with it.

Many traditional time management programs do not take personal work styles into account. They don't help you understand why you are—or aren't— acting productively. Instead, they preach generic time management "solutions." This one-size-fits-all approach can be counterproductive for many people.

If you have tried to implement any of these "traditional" techniques only to fail, the fault may not be yours. For example, many books tell you to touch a piece of paper only once. Depending on your decision-making style, this kind of "advice" may hinder rather than help you. Worse, if you try this approach and it doesn't work, you may believe that the fault is yours—that "something is wrong with you." Rather than beating yourself up, you need to understand your decision-making style and determine whether it serves you. If it does, there's no need to change. If it doesn't serve you, you need strategies that do work for you—and not necessarily the "traditional" ones.

Ask for questions.

OBJECTIVES FOR MODULE 1 (5 MINUTES)

Show Overhead 1.2: Objectives for Module 1.

> *Objectives for Module 1*
>
> - Understand the difference between time management and productivity
> - Identify how you currently spend time.
> - Identify and eliminate time wasters.
> - Create goals to support essential job functions.
> - Plan to improve productivity.
>
> 1.2

Commentary

How many people feel that their time is out of control? That they don't have enough hours in the day to get things done? Ask for a show of hands.

Our goals for this module are to help you:

- Understand the difference between time management and productivity. As I mentioned earlier, time management and productivity do not necessarily go together. Time management is a tool to make you more productive. It can help you:
  - Identify what's important so that you spend your time on primary activities that produce the most results.
  - Reduce stress.
  - Create balance between work and nonwork activities.
  - Deliver better customer service by responding more efficiently to customer needs.

- Identify how you currently spend your time. Where does your time go now? Are you spending it on the right things and getting them done? Or are you scattered and unfocused?

- Identify time wasters and create strategies for eliminating them. What wastes your time, and what can you do about it?

- Set goals and create plans to support them. Doing a few of the right things is more important and more productive than doing many of the wrong things.

- Plan your time and use your plan to get things done. We'll learn how to create plans that support your goals and help you become more productive.

WHERE DOES YOUR TIME GO? (10 MINUTES)

Facilitator: Distribute Handout 1.1: Sample Time Log and Handout 1.2: Time Log.

SAMPLE TIME LOG

Instructions: List each activity you do for two weeks to find out where your time goes. Enter the date, a brief description of the activity, the time you began and ended it, and a ranking for its importance. Rank an activity from 5 to 1, with 5 for the activities critical to your success and 1 for activities that contribute little to your success. Keep your log for at least two weeks. At the end of the two weeks, analyze the log to see where your time goes and develop strategies for streamlining activities, eliminating time wasters, and becoming more productive.

Date	Activity	Time Started/Ended	Rank
8/9	Up/shower/breakfast	5:30 A.M./5:45 A.M.	N/A
	Commute	5:45 A.M./6:45 A.M.	N/A
	Breakfast meeting with clients	6:45 A.M./7:30 A.M.	4
	Travel to office	7:30 A.M./8:00 A.M.	N/A
	Returned emails	8:00 A.M./8:35 A.M.	3
	Retrieved voicemails	8:35 A.M./8:45 A.M.	3
	Returned voicemails	8:45 A.M./9:25 A.M.	3
	Began writing ABC proposal	9:25 A.M./10:20 A.M.	4
	Answered phone call	10:20 A.M./10:25 A.M.	2
	Interrupted by employee with questions about procedures	10:25 A.M./10:40 A.M.	2
	Continued writing ABC proposal	10:40 A.M./12:05 P.M.	4
	Lunch	12:05 P.M./1:15 P.M.	N/A
	Returned emails	1:15 P.M./1:35 P.M.	3
	Retrieved voicemails	1:35 P.M./1:45 P.M.	3
	Returned voicemails	1:45 P.M./2:25 P.M.	3
	Meeting on new marketing project	2:30 P.M./4:45 P.M.	4
	Returned emails	4:50 P.M./5:00 P.M.	3
	Retrieved voicemails	5:00 P.M./5:10 P.M.	3
	Returned voicemails	5:10 P.M./5:35 P.M.	3
	Commute	5:45 P.M./7:15 P.M.	N/A

Date	Activity	Time Started/Ended	Rank
	Exercise	7:15 P.M./8:00 P.M.	4
	Dinner/family time	8:00 P.M./9:30 P.M.	5
	Work on monthly report	9:30 P.M./10:45 P.M.	3
	Time Log evaluation	10:45 P.M./11:00 P.M.	N/A
	Bed	11:00 P.M.	N/A

Time Log Evaluation

- How satisfied are you with your day? *Moderately*
- How much time did you spend on the most important activities (those you rated 4s or 5s)? *7.5 hours*
- How much time did you spend on less important activities? *4.75 hours*
- Was your day balanced? *Pretty much*
- Did you take action on your most important goals? *Yes*

TIME LOG

Instructions: List each activity you do for two weeks to find out where your time goes. Enter the date, a brief description of the activity, the time you began and ended it, and a ranking for its importance. Rank an activity from 5 to 1, with 5 for activities critical to your success and 1 for activities that contribute little to your success. Keep your log for at least two weeks. At the end of the two weeks, analyze the log to see where your time goes and develop strategies for streamlining activities, eliminating time wasters, and becoming more productive.

Date	Activity	Time Started/Ended	Rank

Date	Activity	Time Started/Ended	Rank

Time Log Evaluation
- How satisfied are you with your day?
- How much time did you spend on the most important activities?
- How much time did you spend on less important activities?
- Was your day balanced?
- Did you take action on your most important goals?

Commentary

We're going to start this module by finding out where your time goes. The best way to do this is to complete a time log. Handout 1.1 is a Sample Time Log.

Has anyone ever completed a time log before?

Group Discussion

Ask for a show of hands. Call on one to three people and ask them to share their experiences with the class. If the experiences were positive, ask how keeping the log helped them become more productive. If the experiences were negative, ask them what would have made the activity more helpful. Then call on someone who can share a positive experience, so that the discussion ends on an upbeat note. Integrate the responses into your commentary, where appropriate.

Commentary

Here's how a time log works. You list each activity you perform to find out where your time goes. You enter the date, a brief description of the activity, the time you began and ended it, and a ranking for its importance. You rank an activity from 5 to 1, with 5 for the most important activities and 1 for the least important. Answer the questions at the end of the log at the end of each day.

It's best to keep your log for at least two weeks. At the end of two weeks, analyze the log to see where your time goes and develop strategies for streamlining activities, eliminating time wasters, and becoming more productive. Identify where you need to create procedures for repetitive tasks and projects.

Look at Handout 1.1: Sample Time Log. Note that this person handles emails and voicemails three times a day. That may make sense for her, but it may not make sense for you. Depending on your job, handling emails once a day may be more productive. Or, you may have to respond to them as they arrive in your mailbox.

Identifying similar activities and clustering them can save time. In this example, setting aside blocks of time to answer correspondence, handle phone calls and emails, and make photocopies can help this person handle these tasks faster and more easily.

You can see that this person is interrupted by an employee who has questions about procedures. If entries such as this one appear frequently on your time log, it may mean that that employee needs training. Or you may need to create a procedures manual so employees do not constantly interrupt you with questions they could find the answers to elsewhere.

Can you begin to see how valuable a time log can be? How much information it can give you?

We can't complete a time log now, but I encourage you to begin one when you return to your office. You can copy Handout 1.2 and use it more than once. This is the best way to identify where your time goes and put into place strategies that can make you more productive. We'll talk about many of these strategies as we go through the program. In the meantime, let's do a quick survey of where your time goes by listing some of the activities you perform each day.

Group Discussion

Lead a group discussion and have participants identify where their time goes. Who spends a lot of time on the phone? Incoming calls? Outgoing calls? Both? What about emails? Do you spend time at meetings? What are some other activities that take up your time during the day?

As you can see, we spend our time doing a wide variety of activities, not all of which directly contribute the most to productivity.

IDENTIFYING TIME WASTERS (20 MINUTES)
Commentary

Only your time log can tell you where your time is being wasted, but we can look at some common time wasters and decide how we can reduce or eliminate them.

Team Activity: Targeting Time Wasters

 Facilitator: Distribute Handout 1.3: Identifying Time Wasters.

Working with your team, choose three time wasters from this list or select ones not on the list that are a challenge for you. Identify at least three ways you can reduce or eliminate each of these time wasters. When you are finished, we'll share some of your strategies with the entire group. You have fifteen minutes for this exercise.

Ask for questions.

Debriefing: Ask as many teams as there is time to discuss one of their time wasters and the strategies they came up with.

Break: Take a five-minute stretch break. Then call the room to order.

IDENTIFYING TIME WASTERS

Instructions: Choose three of these time wasters—or some of your own—and working with your team, create three strategies for reducing or eliminating them.

1. How can I find files/papers faster?

2. How can I use voicemail to get things done?

3. How can I make decisions more quickly?

4. How can I get people to follow instructions better?

5. How can I meet deadlines more often?

6. How can I make my work space more efficient?

7. How can I better prioritize tasks?

8. How can I make myself throw out things I don't use and no longer need?

9. How can I handle my mail?

10. How can I make sure people call me back?

11. How can I get to the bottom of my in-box every day?

12. Other:

IDENTIFYING AND SETTING GOALS (30 MINUTES)
Commentary

Who is familiar with the 80/20 rule? Ask for a show of hands and a volunteer to explain the 80/20 rule.

The 80/20 rule is also called the Pareto Principle. It states that 80 percent of our major achievements are accomplished in just 20 percent of our time. The rule works when we in fact spend 20 percent of our time doing what counts, doing activities with the highest value.

If the 80/20 rule is true, we should have all the time we need to accomplish what is most important for us. So why aren't we all high achievers? Because we spend more time on less important activities than we should. We get caught in time traps.

When you complete your time log, you'll discover where your time traps are, where your time goes. Many of you will discover that you spend 80 percent of your time on only 20 percent of what's most important. You're too busy to be productive!

So, how do you turn this around? The strategies in this workshop will teach you how to master the 80/20 rule.

Remember: Effort does not automatically produce results. In fact, hard work may have a negative effect on productivity since hard work depletes your energy and erodes your enthusiasm. Often, the harder you work, the less you want to work, and the less you produce.

One of the keys to improving productivity is to spend time in high-quality activities that produce the most results. Often, these activities challenge you and excite you. They rev up your energy, not enervate you, and your enthusiasm improves productivity. Goals have great power. All your goals together provide a direction for your work and your life. So, what are your most important goals? What activities are critical to your success? Which activities contribute the most to your career and company?

Having clearly defined goals helps you to focus on what's important. It gives you a long-term vision that helps you prioritize activities and concentrate on the key 20 percent that produces 80 percent of results. There are several advantages in setting goals.

 Show Overhead 1.3: The Value of Goals.

> **The Value of Goals**
>
> You can:
> • Measure progress.
> • Reduce stress.
> • Develop self-confidence.
> • Become a star performer.
>
> _____
> 1.3   © 2001 Patricia Haddock.

Commentary

When you create goals, you can:

• See and measure your progress toward achieving what you want. This provides motivation and stimulus to keep going. It gets you over the hard parts.

- Reduce stress and tension because you always know where you are with regard to your goals.

- Develop the self-confidence that comes from achieving what you want in your work and life.

- Become a star performer who gets the right things done and creates positive results.

Goals give you structure, a reason for doing certain things or not doing them. They provide criteria against which you can make decisions.

Right now, we're concentrating on career/work goals, but you should set goals for all areas of your life—not just career, but also education, relationships, family, finances, health, and fitness. We'll cover many of these areas later in Module 8: Creating Balance and Setting Boundaries.

 Show Overhead 1.4: SMART Goals.

> **SMART Goals**
>
> Specific: Spell out each goal in detail.
> Measurable: You need to evaluate success.
> Adaptable: Goals need to respond to what's happening in your life.
> Realistic: Blue sky, but be real!
> Timely: Put a deadline on each goal.
>
> 1.4   © 2001 Patricia Haddock.

Goals should be SMART:

- Specific. Clearly spell out steps that contribute most to the performance of that goal.

- Measurable. Establish criteria by which you can evaluate the goal and determine when you have achieved it.

- Adaptable. Goals must be flexible and respond to personal, professional, business, and environmental changes.

- Realistic. Blue sky, but keep both feet on the ground. Set goals that stretch and grow your abilities, but aren't so difficult that you become discouraged.

- Timely. Put a deadline on each goal.

Individual Exercise: Identifying Your Major Goals

 Facilitator: Distribute Handout 1.4: Doing What's Most Important.

Instructions to Participants: In this exercise, you are going to identify your top three major goals for your career. What must you achieve in order to ensure your success? What do you, personally, want to achieve in your career? For example, among your top three goals might be to become a partner in your company or start your own business. Another top major goal might be to obtain a graduate degree in your field. After you list your goals, decide how

DOING WHAT'S MOST IMPORTANT

Instructions: Identify your top three career goals. What must you accomplish in order to ensure your success? Prioritize your goals from most important to least important. While all of these goals are important, establishing priorities will help you make better decisions and set smaller goals to accomplish what's most important.

Goal	Priority
1.	
2.	
3.	

important each one is, ranking the most important goal as "1," the next most important as "2," and the last goal as "3."

List your top three goals for your job on Handout 1.4. You have ten minutes for this exercise.

Ask for questions.

> *Facilitator: Circulate among participants as they work on this exercise. If anyone seems to be having a problem, solicit questions from him or her to help clarify the exercise.*

Commentary

In order for you to meet your major goals, you must set certain smaller goals that are stepping stones to your major goals. Goals should always be meaningful and provide a sense of pride at their accomplishment. Setting the right goals will ensure that you spend 20 percent of your time accomplishing 80 percent of the results. For example, if you want to start your own business in five years, a long-term goal might be to get your MBA in entrepreneurship from a major university four years from now. A mid-term goal might be to write a book to establish your expertise in two years. A short-term goal might be to research MBA programs and apply to one within the next nine months.

Individual Exercise: Setting SMART Goals

> *Facilitator: Distribute Handout 1.5: Setting SMART Goals and Handout 1.6: Sample Setting SMART Goals.*

Instructions to Participants: Take your top-priority goal from the previous exercise and define three key smaller goals: (1) a long-term goal to be met within the next three to five years, (2) a mid-term goal to be met within the next one to three years, and (3) a short-term goal to be met within the next twelve months. Each of your goals will break down into smaller SMART goals until you have a to-do list of activities and tasks that are critical to your success. At each step you also prioritize your goals, so you know which is the most important at every step in the process. By concentrating on these activities, you will be spending time on the 20 percent that produces 80 percent of the results.

Make sure goals allow you to stretch and grow. The Japanese concept of *kaizen* teaches us to make continuous improvement. Little continuous improvements, added together, may have a greater impact than a major change introduced all at once. Where can you make small changes so that you can spend more of your time on the 20 percent that makes the most difference? Keep the concept of *kaizen* in mind when you are creating your goals. You have ten minutes for this exercise.

Ask for questions.

SETTING SMART GOALS

Instructions: Take your top-priority goal and define three key smaller goals—a long-term goal to be met within the next three to five years; a mid-term goal to be met within the next one to three years, and a short-term goal to be met within the next twelve months. (Transfer each goal in the short-term column to Handout 1.6: Planning to Reach Your Goals.) Break each goal down into smaller SMART goals until you end up with a to-do list of activities and tasks.

Top-Priority Goal:

Long-Term Goal (3–5 years)	Mid-Term Goal (1–3 years)	Short-Term Goal (12 months)

- Is each goal SMART?
- What resources/training/help do you need to achieve this goal?
- Is this the right goal, or will another goal take you toward your objective faster and more easily?

SAMPLE SET OF SMART GOALS

Let's say that one of your top-priority goals is to start your own business in four years. Here's how your chart would look.

Top-Priority Goal: Start your own business

Long-Term Goal (3–5 years)	Mid-Term Goal (1–3 years)	Short-Term Goal (12 months)
Get my MBA in entrepreneurship.	Start program one year from now.	Research MBA programs within the next 6 weeks. Obtain information about likely programs within the next 3 months. Apply to likely programs within the next 6 months.

Transfer each goal in the Short-Term Goal column to Handout 1.6: Planning to Reach Your Goals and create smaller and smaller action steps.

Facilitator: Circulate among participants as they work on this exercise. If anyone seems to be having a problem, solicit questions from him or her to help clarify the exercise.

Commentary

Just setting goals isn't enough. You must commit to achieving them. Set dates on your calendar to review your progress and determine whether you need to change your goals. Evaluate how well you have done at each deadline. Did you reach your goals? Yes? Take time to reward yourself for your accomplishment; then set new goals that raise the bar. Remember the principle of *kaizen*.

Did you not reach your goal? Why not? What got in the way? Is it the right goal? Do you still want to achieve this goal? If so, what can you do to rectify the situation? One major reason for failing to achieve goals is failing to plan.

Ask for questions.

PLANNING TO IMPROVE PRODUCTIVITY (20 MINUTES)
Commentary

Achieving your major goals by setting and reaching smaller goals requires planning. Planning is a process to identify the most effective way of getting what you want when you want it.

Show Overhead 1.5: The Benefits of Planning.

Planning helps you:

- Anticipate challenges and develop strategies for overcoming them.
- Stay on track and on target.
- Spend time on the most productive activities.
- Focus on critical activities.
- Gather needed resources.
- Identify how much effort and expense will be required.

The Benefits of Planning

Planning helps you:
- Anticipate challenges.
- Stay on target.
- Be more productive.
- Focus on critical activities.
- Gather needed resources.
- Identify effort and expense.

1.5

Individual Exercise: Planning to Reach Your Goals

 Facilitator: Distribute Handout 1.7: Planning to Reach Your Goals.

Commentary

Look at the goals you wrote on Handout 1.5. Write your short-term goal on Handout 1.7: Planning to Reach Your Goals. Identify all the action steps you need to take. What resources do you need? You may have to break large actions down into a series of smaller actions and tasks. Set deadlines for each action and task and prioritize them.

When estimating how much time a task/project will take, consider:

- Other high-priority/urgent tasks
- Emergencies and illnesses
- Meetings
- Time off, i.e., vacations
- Equipment failure
- People failure
- Quality issues and errors

The process of prioritizing action steps helps create a plan. Look at each action step and decide how much time you need to accomplish that step. You have ten minutes for this exercise.

Ask for questions.

 Facilitator: Circulate among participants as they work on this exercise. If anyone seems to be having a problem, solicit questions from him or her to help clarify the exercise.

Commentary

You now have created a plan to achieve this goal. You need to do this for every goal. After you have a plan for each goal, ask these questions:

- Will the plan work? If not, how can you make it work?
- How much will the plan cost in resources and expenses? Is the cost worth it?
- Are there conflicts with plans for other goals? If so, how can the conflicts be resolved?

The last step is to implement the plan. Enter action steps and tasks on your calendar, and make appointments with yourself to get things done. Always

PLANNING TO REACH YOUR GOALS

Instructions: Take your top-priority short-term goal from Handout 1.5 and write it here. Identify all the action steps that need to be taken to reach this goal.

Top-Priority Short-Term Goal:

Action Steps	Time Required	Deadline	Resources Needed

plan to accomplish the most important tasks each day. Using a calendar system—paper or electronic—is critical to the success of your plan.

Paper calendars should be easy to use and carry and should suit your personality. They range from simple to very elaborate. Some allow you to create and keep project and meeting records. Computer planners do what paper planners do and more. It's easy to reschedule activities and schedule group activities. Some offer contact software features so you can call and fax from your calendar software.

Plan your week on Sunday; then spend time each day evaluating how well you have done and going over what you need to do the next day. Planning on a weekly basis can help you reach your goals more easily than if you do just daily planning.

Make appointments with yourself to work on key projects. Set a goal to accomplish the most important tasks each day. What's most important may change during the course of the day as situations change and emergencies arise. Sometimes, it may make sense to shift your emphasis as the day progresses, especially if your work requires creativity, which is difficult to call up on demand.

Never completely book your day. Leave some open time in your schedule for interruptions and emergencies. You also need time for unstructured activities. Creativity, brainstorming, and problem solving often are most fruitful if they are unstructured and free-flowing. Be willing to drop little things to stay on track.

Take your personal work styles into account. For example, if you are a morning person, schedule important appointments and set aside time to make decisions early in the day when you are fresh. Reverse this if you are a night person and don't reach your peak until later in the day. Perform more routine tasks such as returning calls and answering correspondence in the afternoon. You'll learn more about work styles in Module 5: Understanding Work Styles.

Some people rebel at planning their day with such rigor. You may prefer to go with the flow and let your intuition guide you. If this works for you and you are productive, there's no need to change. Just make sure you monitor your progress for your major goals. If this free-flowing approach to planning isn't working, you need to impose some discipline and plan at least part of your day to ensure you are moving toward your goals.

Keep your goals where you can see them and review them daily. Ask yourself if each activity is necessary to achieve your goals. Is this the most important activity you should be doing? Is this the best time to do this activity?

Confirm appointments the day before. When scheduling time for appointments, build in travel time and consider the work style of the person you are meeting with. A good rule is to add fifteen to thirty minutes to the amount of time you think the appointment will take. This additional time will accommodate people who need time for relationship building and more personal interaction.

If you arrive early, have a "to-read" file handy so you don't waste waiting time. You'll learn about "to-read" files in Module 2: Getting Organized. If you are kept waiting more than fifteen minutes, consider rescheduling the meeting and leaving.

Use a daily to-do list to help you keep track of things that need your attention but that don't need to be scheduled on your calendar. Errands and routine chores should be on your to-do list, but don't let your to-do list become a shopping list of sixty-eight items you will never accomplish. Keep your to-do list manageable. Some time management experts recommend that you have no more than seven items on your list at one time. Don't add to your list until you scratch items off because they are done or you have decided not to do them.

You also need a tickler system. Your calendar system may have one built into it. If not, set up seven file folders labeled for each day of the week—Sunday, Monday, Tuesday, Wednesday, Thursday, Friday, Saturday. Drop a note into the appropriate folder as a reminder to follow up on that day. Review each day's file the evening before.

For a long-term tickler system, set up twelve folders, one for each month. Review each folder at the beginning of the month. For example, if your insurance premium notice arrives in June and payment isn't due until the end of August, put a reminder to pay the premium in the August folder. On August 1, review the contents of the August file and move reminders into the appropriate day-of-the-week folder. In this example, if I decide to mail the insurance payment on the last Monday of the month, I will put a reminder in the Monday folder to do so.

Your plan will probably take time to accomplish since some of your goals are five years away! Often, people grow impatient and feel frustrated when the realization of important goals is so far away. The key to persistence is contained in your mid-term and short-term goals. Achieving these goals provides you with milestones and proof that you are on the right track to achieving your long-term goals. When you achieve a goal, make sure you reward yourself for your achievement.

Ask for questions.

Break: We're going to take a fifteen-minute break now. Please return at [time]. We will start the next module promptly.

Administrative Details—Notes

Objectives

Your Time Management Problems	What time management problems do you hope to solve by the end of the workshop?

Time Management vs. Productivity—Notes

Objectives for Module 1	
Where Does Your Time Go?	List some of the activities you perform each day:
Identifying Time Wasters	
Identifying and Setting Goals	Why are goals valuable?
Planning to Improve Productivity	What are the benefits of planning?

Getting Organized (2 Hours)

OBJECTIVES FOR MODULE 2
- Understand and apply principles of organization.
- Clear clutter and create order.
- Understand and apply filing strategies.
- Organize the work space for greater productivity and efficiency.

MATERIALS NEEDED
- Handout 2.1: Review Module 1
- Handout 2.2: Setting Organization Goals
- Handout 2.3: Sort and Toss Checklist
- Handout 2.4: Checklist for Filing Success
- Handout 2.5: Setting Up Files
- Handout 2.6: How Do You Handle These Environmental Challenges?
- Handout 2.7: Organize These Items
- Handout 2.8: Telephone Dos and Don'ts
- Handout 2.9: Email Dos and Don'ts
- Handout 2.10: Checklist for Managing Computer Files and Software
- Overhead 2.1: Getting Organized

- Overhead 2.2: Objectives for Module 2
- Overhead 2.3: Principles of Organization
- Overhead 2.4: Sort and Toss Session
- Overhead 2.5: What to Keep
- Overhead 2.6: Filing Strategies
- Overhead 2.7: Sample File Categories
- Overhead 2.8: Organizing Your Work Space
- Overhead 2.9: Organize These Items
- Overhead 2.10: Managing Phones
- Overhead 2.11: Managing Email
- Overhead 2.12: Managing Computer Files and Software

AGENDA

Review Module 1	15 minutes
Getting Organized	5 minutes
Objectives for Module 2	5 minutes
Principles of Organization	15 minutes
Clearing Clutter and Creating Order	15 minutes
Creating a Filing System So You Can Find Things	25 minutes
Organizing the Work Space	20 minutes
Managing Phones and Email	10 minutes
Managing Computer Files and Software	10 minutes

REVIEW MODULE 1 (15 MINUTES)

 Facilitator: Welcome people back. Distribute Handout 2.1: Review Module 1.

Individual Exercise: Applying Lessons from Module 1

Before we start the next module on getting organized, let's think about what we learned in Module 1: Time Management and Productivity. Determine the three most important things you learned from the first module, and commit to three action items to improve productivity when you return to your office. You have fifteen minutes for this exercise.

INTRODUCE MODULE 2: GETTING ORGANIZED (5 MINUTES)

 Facilitator: Call the room to order and ask for two or three people to share what they learned.

 Show Overhead 2.1: Getting Organized.

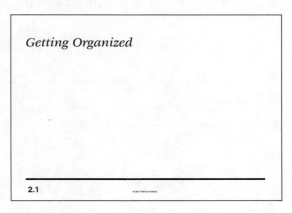

Commentary

For some people, being organized comes naturally. No stacks clutter their work space. Their desk is clear and neat. They can find things instantly. For other people, disorder is the order of the day. They seem to thrive in clutter, and even though everything looks messy, they usually manage to find what they need. Still others have offices that look like a hurricane blew through. What's worse, they are so disorganized, they can't find anything.

Some people judge our competence by the condition of our work area. They think that people with messy work spaces are less competent than those who are neat and organized. This may not be fair, but perception is reality, and being disorganized can, in fact, lead to unprofessional behavior.

Have you ever forgotten to return a phone call, lost an important file or document, or misfiled papers you need? Have you ever misplaced completed work, requiring you to redo it, or spent hours looking for something in your office only to find it at home on your dining room table? If you answered "yes" to any of these situations, disorganization is not only negatively impacting your productivity—your professional image is suffering.

According to organization experts, approximately 80 percent of people say they want to be more organized. Becoming organized can give you more time,

REVIEW MODULE 1

Instructions: Determine the three most important things you learned from Module 1: Time Management and Productivity. Commit to three action items to improve productivity when you return to your desk.

Most important things learned in Module 1:

1. _____

2. _____

3. _____

Action items to improve productivity:

1. _____

2. _____

3. _____

help you to create a professional image, and allow you to adapt to changing situations.

But just getting organized isn't enough. You need to focus on keeping things current. You do this by setting up procedures and standards for maintaining order. The goal is to get organized and stay organized so you can find what you need quickly and easily.

OBJECTIVES FOR MODULE 2 (5 MINUTES)

 Show Overhead 2.2: Objectives for Module 2.

> *Objectives for Module 2*
>
> • Understand and apply principles of organization.
> • Understand filing strategies.
> • Eliminate clutter.
> • Create order.
> • Organize your work space.
>
> 2.2

Commentary

This module will teach you principles and strategies for getting and staying organized. You will learn how to:

- Understand and apply principles of organization.
- Understand and apply filing strategies.
- Eliminate clutter.
- Create and maintain order.
- Organize your work space for greater productivity and efficiency.

For many of us, a few preliminary steps are required before we can get organized. Sometimes, we think that we don't have time to get organized. And in fact, if you tackled everything that needs to be organized, it could take several days of dedicated activity. No one can devote that much time to getting organized. On the other hand, failing to get organized means lost productivity every day. The solution is, as usual, moderation. Devote fifteen minutes, half an hour, or an hour a day to getting organized. Take small steps, and eventually, you will have accomplished the task. You'll be able to find things more quickly and easily, your productivity and efficiency will improve, and so will your self-esteem.

Some of us can't get organized because we're so disorganized we don't know where to start. One solution is to start with an area that will have the greatest impact on your productivity and/or self-esteem when it is organized. For many people, this is their desk.

Sometimes, instead of your desk, it makes sense to start with storage areas such as cabinets, closets, and bookcases. By organizing storage areas, you free up space to house material from the areas you subsequently organize.

Wherever you decide to begin, the most important thing is to start somewhere. Tackle one drawer, one shelf, one surface—but just begin.

Ask for questions.

PRINCIPLES OF ORGANIZATION (15 MINUTES)

 Show Overhead 2.3: Principles of Organization.

┌─────────────────────────────────────┐
│ *Principles of Organization*   │
│   │
│ • Organize to support your goals.   │
│ • Designate a place for everything, and keep everything │
│   in its place.   │
│ • Honor your personal style.   │
│   │
│ ─────────────────────────────────   │
│ **2.3**   │
└─────────────────────────────────────┘

Commentary

There are three basic principles of organization:

1. Organize to support your goals.

2. Designate a place for everything, and keep everything in its place.

3. Honor your personal style.

If you follow these three principles, you will create and maintain order.

When you organize to support your goals, you improve your productivity. Think about one area of your work space right now. It could be your desk, your credenza, the floor of your work space. Does this area support your goals, or does it get in the way of meeting your goals?

Group Discussion

Let's talk about how being organized can help you reach your goals. How does organization contribute to your success?

 Facilitator: Lead a group discussion, listing answers on a flipchart or whiteboard. Encourage responses on the importance of creating files, of maintaining a neat work area, and of labeling information for easy retrieval.

Individual Exercise: Setting Organization Goals

 Facilitator: Distribute Handout 2.2: Setting Organization Goals.

Instructions to Participants: You will need to refer to the following handouts from Module 1 during the exercise:

SETTING ORGANIZATION GOALS

Instructions: Identify your top three organization goals and rank them from most important to least important.

Objective	Priority
1.	
2.	
3.	

- Handout 1.4: Doing What's Most Important
- Handout 1.5: Setting SMART Goals
- Handout 1.6: Planning to Reach Your Goals

Review the handouts you completed in Module 1. Now, decide your top three goals for getting organized. Remember, goals must be SMART.

Ask for a participant to define what SMART goals are.

Ask for questions.

You have ten minutes for this exercise.

 Facilitator: Call the room to order and ask for two to three people to share the organization goals they set.

CLEARING CLUTTER AND CREATING ORDER (15 MINUTES)
Commentary

When we talk about creating a place for everything and keeping everything in its place, we aren't trying to impose a rigid structure. Rather, we're suggesting that you create and use a consistent structure, that you set up a system that works for you and suits your personality. One size does not fit all.

Many people find that traditional strategies and time management tools don't work because they don't fit their organization styles. There is no single solution for everyone. You have to try different ways of organizing until you find what works for you and stick to that. The key is to keep improving and becoming more efficient using methods that work for you.

For many people, another adage holds true: "Out of sight, out of mind." Once they file something away, they forget about it. These people are often highly visual. They remember where things are and locate things by what they look like and where they are in relation to other things. One solution is open shelving. Another solution is to house files in various places depending on usage. For example, files needed for phone calls can be kept near the phone. Project files can be assigned special areas on the top of the credenza or shelved in the bookcase. If you are visual and need to keep papers and files in sight, keep them neat and orderly. If it takes you more than a few minutes to find something, your files are out of control. You can also create a visual map of where you have filed things and always use your tickler system to remind yourself that you need to take action.

In order to be organized, you have to *get* organized. If you're like many people, you have stacks of papers that need to be sorted before you can see your desktop, let alone maintain order.

Clutter is emotionally draining and causes delays, frustration, and stress. Facing a mess every day can make you feel irritable and tired before you even begin the day. Experts estimate that we spend about 150 hours a year looking for misplaced information and items. That's about one full month of lost productivity.

Show Overhead 2.4: Sort and Toss Session.

 Facilitator: Distribute Handout 2.3: Sort and Toss Checklist.

> **Sort and Toss Session**
>
> - Create one or more piles
> - Act
> - Recycle or toss
>   - File
>   - Decide
>   - Respond
>   - Read
>
> 2.4

Commentary

Start clearing the clutter with a "Sort and Toss Session." If you don't have time to sort and toss all the stacks of paper in your office, start by sorting and tossing for fifteen minutes a day. Set a goal to clear one stack a week until all the clutter is gone. Once you eliminate the stacks, start on the drawers, filing cabinets, and bookcases.

Follow this procedure as you sort and toss:

- Create one or more piles of everything that doesn't have a place or isn't in its place. Include everything that is piled on the top of furniture, on the floor, or anywhere it doesn't belong.

- Go through each pile from top to bottom, touching each piece of paper once, and ask these questions:

  - Do you need to take action? If so, act now.

  - Do you need this piece of paper again? If you don't need it, recycle it or toss it. If you do need it, where will you file it? Do you already have a file set up for it? If so, immediately file it away. If not, put it in a pile labeled "To Set Up Files." We'll talk about setting up files later.

  - Can you make a decision on this paper now, or do you need more information? If you can make a decision, do so. If you need more information, where will you file this paper before you make a decision? How will you get the information you need? How will you remember that it is an open item that needs resolution? Do you need a system for following up and closing open items?

  - Do you need to respond? If so, how and when will you respond?

  - Do you need to read this? Is this information still relevant? If it is more than six months old, consider tossing it. Store things you need to read in a "to-read" file, sorted by oldest to most current, and carry it with you. Never put entire magazines in your to-read file. When you get a magazine, go through it and tear out the articles you want to read. Note the source and date of the publication on the article, and then recycle or toss the rest of the magazine in the trash. Make it a habit to read clippings from this file when you are waiting for meetings to begin, on public transportation, and in small pockets of time that are too small to tackle a major project.

SORT AND TOSS CHECKLIST

❏ Create piles of everything that doesn't have a place or isn't in its place.

❏ Go through each pile from top to bottom, touching each piece of paper once, and ask these questions:

 ❏ Do you need to take action? If so, act now.

 ❏ Do you need this piece of paper again? If you don't need it, recycle it or toss it. If you do need it, where will you file it? Do you already have a file set up for it? If so, immediately file it away. If not, put it in a pile labeled "To Set Up Files."

 ❏ Can you make a decision now, or do you need more information? If you can make a decision, do so. If you need more information, where will you file this paper before you make a decision? How will you get the information you need?

 ❏ Do you need to respond? If so, how and when will you respond?

 ❏ Do you need to read this? Is this information still relevant? If it is more than six months old, consider tossing it. Store things you need to read in a "to-read" file, sorted by oldest to most current, and carry it with you. Make it a habit to read required information when you are waiting for a meeting to begin, on public transportation, and in small pockets of time that are too small to tackle a major project.

Show Overhead 2.5: What to Keep.

> **What to Keep**
>
> • Hard-to-replace items
> • Legally required documents
> • Documentation
> • Originals
>
> _____
> 2.5

Commentary

Some people have a hard time throwing things out. What is the worst thing that could happen if you throw out an item and need it later? Keep something only if it is worth saving and if:

- It would be difficult to get another copy.
- Retention for a period of time is required by law or for tax purposes.
- You need it for an ongoing project or documentation.
- You originated the document.

Keep in mind that almost everything is replaceable. Toss or recycle an item if:

- It is no longer current or relevant.
- You refer to it infrequently.
- It adds nothing new to information you are already keeping.
- You don't have time to read it and won't miss the information.
- Someone else has the information, and you personally don't really need to keep it.
- You won't refer to it again.
- You can get a copy if you need it.
- You don't need it.

Make it easy to throw things away by keeping your wastebasket, recycle bin, or shredder handy. Use them often and resist the urge to retrieve items from the trash.

Ask for questions.

Break: Take a five-minute stretch break.

CREATING A FILING SYSTEM SO YOU CAN FIND THINGS (25 MINUTES)

Commentary

When you finish a Sort and Toss Session, you should have disposed of every piece of paper. Now, take the folder "To Set Up Files" and create files using the following guidelines.

Show Overhead 2.6: Filing Strategies.

 Facilitator: Distribute Handout 2.4: Checklist for Filing Success.

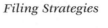

Filing Strategies

- Label files.
- Create a Master List.
- House based on frequency of use.
- Ensure confidentiality.

2.6

Create files using broad headings with subcategories. You can label according to subject, alphabetically, geographically, chronologically, or numerically. For example, a subject head could be "Software." Subcategories within "Software" could be created by vendor name or product name in alphabetical order. Another head could be "Invoices," with subcategories by vendor. Within vendor, each invoice could be organized by date, starting with the most current.

Creating a "Master List" with cross-references can help you locate papers once they are filed. A Master List is like the index of a book. It lists categories and subcategories and is a map to your filing system. A Master List is very important if you are absent and someone else needs to find something in your files.

 Show Overhead 2.7: Sample File Categories.

Commentary

Some people have a hard time narrowing titles to a single heading. For example, "Automobile Insurance" could be filed under "Automobile," "Insurance," the name of the insurance company, or the make and model of the car being insured. For these people, a Master List of filing categories is a must.

Sample File Categories

Insurance
    Allstate
        Liability Policies
           Automobile Policies

2.7

Start by identifying a major category. In this example, let's use "Insurance." Within "Insurance," you can set up subcategories either by type of insurance or name of insurer. If you choose to sort by insurer, within each insurer's name, you would have additional subcategories for types of insurance and other items.

CHECKLIST FOR FILING SUCCESS

❑ Create files using broad headings with subcategories. You can label according to subject, alphabetically, geographically, chronologically, or numerically.

❑ Create a Master List with cross-references.

❑ Keep files you use frequently near your work area, and archive files you rarely use.

❑ Periodically conduct a Sort and Toss Session for each file drawer.

❑ Keep personnel files confidential, with access restricted to authorized people only. Medical information about employees must be filed apart from employment files and be kept confidential with access restricted to authorized people only.

❑ Stop accumulating paper. Use these tips to cut out paper:

- Use the phone, electronic files, and email whenever possible.
- Never put down a piece of paper without doing something to move it along.
- Create files only as needed using the criteria established in this section.
- Send copies to only those people who really need them.
- Set up a place for incoming mail and paper. Empty this in-basket daily using the sort and toss method.
- Set up a place for outgoing mail and paper.
- Set up a "to-file" box and empty it daily.
- Return files to their drawers promptly.
- Label storage boxes for each identification and retrieval.

Group Discussion

Lead a group discussion and pose the following questions to participants:

- Looking at this label system, where would you file claims?
- Where would you file policy updates?
- Where would you file papers related to a lawsuit you have against Allstate?
- What other subcategories of insurance-related information might you have?
- How would you label these files, and where would you put them?

Store files based on frequency of use. Keep files you use frequently in your work area. Archive historical files and files you use occasionally in another area. Periodically conduct a Sort and Toss Session for each file drawer and eliminate what you no longer need.

As mentioned earlier, visual people need to keep files in sight. As long as you can find what you need quickly and don't have to dig through piles to get your hands on it, your system serves you. If you file project folders away, keep a note about the project visible so you don't forget it. You can also add a note to your weekly or monthly tickler system. A corkboard can become a colorful map of where you have filed things.

Remember that personnel files must be kept confidential, with access restricted to authorized people only. Medical information about employees must be filed apart from employment files and be kept confidential with access restricted to authorized people only.

One key to mastering your system is to stop adding paper to it. Use these tips to cut out paper:

- Use the phone, electronic files, and email whenever possible.
- Never put down a piece of paper without doing something to move it along.
- Create files only as needed using the criteria established in this section.
- Send copies of documents to only those people who really need them.
- Set up a place for incoming mail and paper. Empty this in-basket daily using the sort and toss method.
- Set up a place for outgoing mail and paper.
- Set up a "to-file" box, and empty it daily.
- Return files to their drawers or folders promptly.
- Label storage boxes for easy identification and retrieval.

Ask for questions.

Team Activity: Setting Up Files

 Facilitator: Distribute Handout 2.5: Setting Up Files.

Instructions to Participants: Work within your team and decide how to set up files for the items listed on this handout. You have fifteen minutes for this exercise.

 Facilitator: Call the room to order.

Debriefing: Go around the room and ask each team to share how they categorized and filed one of the items on the list.

 Facilitator: Bring the room to order.

As you can see from this exercise, there are a number of ways a single item can be categorized and filed. A filing system that makes sense for one person may confuse someone else. That's why a Master List is so important.

ORGANIZING THE WORK SPACE (20 MINUTES)

 Show Overhead 2.8: Organizing Your Work Space.

> *Organizing Your Work Space*
>
> • Primary work space
> • Secondary work space
> • Functional and comfortable
>
> 2.8

Commentary

Since you spend at least eight hours a day on your job, your work space needs to be both functional and comfortable. It should be a place you enjoy working in. If customers and vendors meet with you in your cubicle or office or if you hold meetings at your desk, it is important that you maintain an ordered, professional image.

A work space that's conducive to productivity:

- Has good lighting
- Is ergonomically correct
- Has the right equipment for the job
- Has working equipment

SETTING UP FILES

Set up files for these items, and identify major and subcategories of files for each:

- An invoice from Fred's Software Store for Office 2000
- An invoice from WaterWorks for bottled water
- A clipping from a newspaper about the growth of The Community Bank, one of your customers
- A magazine interview with your CEO, Jan Carson, about Widget 2010, which your company just introduced
- A signed contract for a vendor, Madison Temp, to provide temporary agency staff
- An employment application for Cathy Morris, who was hired for a sales job
- A letter of complaint about a defective widget from a customer, Wilson Winkler
- A stack of correspondence about an ongoing project to introduce Widget 3000
- Meeting records from the monthly staff meeting
- A brochure about an upcoming team-building workshop the CEO wants key people to attend

- Offers some privacy
- Minimizes distractions
- Is easy to work in
- Is decorated appropriately for the work being done
- Looks professional
- Reflects the company image
- Is safe

Most people have two work areas to organize: (1) primary work space, which is your desk; and (2) secondary work spaces—credenza, bookcases, file cabinets, etc. In general, you want to organize your space so everything you need is easy to reach from your desk. You also want to place furniture to minimize distractions and discourage visitors from interrupting you. Even if you have no control over how your furniture and computer are set up, you may be able to control how you use and organize your space.

If your work space is not set up for productivity and comfort and you don't have control over how your space is designed, you need to create a plan for changing it. Start with the greatest challenge your work space creates. Your plan should state how this negatively affects your productivity. Include recommendations about how your work space could be changed to improve productivity, and describe the benefits to the company and your department. Present the plan to your manager.

If changes cannot be made, you need to identify how you can change your work habits to work around the challenges. For example, you may be able to work in an empty office, cubicle, or conference room for part of the day, especially if you need to do work that requires concentration such as proofreading, accounting, or auditing. Find out if you can bring a desk lamp to counteract poor lighting or use earplugs to reduce auditory distractions. Make photocopies or run errands when distractions are most intense. Schedule phone calls at times when things are usually quiet.

Team Activity: Handling Environmental Challenges

 Facilitator: Distribute Handout 2.6: How Do You Handle These Environmental Challenges? Assign one or two items from the list to each team.

Instructions to Participants: Work with your team and brainstorm ideas for overcoming the challenges listed on the handout. You have ten minutes for this exercise.

Facilitator: Bring the group to order.

Debriefing: Ask teams to share their solutions.

Commentary

Think about your desk. Where do you do most of your work? Where is your computer located? The area of your desk where you do most of your work is your work center. Think of your work center as high-income property. Everything in the work center should contribute to high returns in productivity.

The general rule is to locate items you use most frequently nearest your work center and items you use less often farther away. To maintain productivity and efficiency, your work center should be kept as clear and organized as you can keep it at all times. When your work center becomes cluttered, immediately take a few minutes to organize it. If you currently have piles in your work center, remove them. Stack them elsewhere or do a quick Sort and Toss Session.

The work center should be empty except for the project you are working on. Make sure you clear your work center before you leave at the end of the day.

Keep your most important personal items at the edges of the work center, and move less important personal items to other areas. Place your calendar on the edge of your work center and keep it open to today's date so you can easily refer to it. If you use an electronic calendar, use a printout of the day's plan.

Put reference items you use often, such as dictionaries and manuals, where you can easily reach them without having to get up. Visual people usually keep more things on their desk—and other surfaces—than other people. If you are visual or if you like to work on more than one project at a time, keep only one file or project in your work center at a time, and make sure you keep files related to each project in a separate project folder. Before you start something new, set aside the file you are currently working on.

After you organize your desktop, do a Sort and Toss Session for the contents of your drawers. Identify what materials and supplies you use all the time. Put desk supplies, such as paper clips, pens, and pencils, in one drawer where you can easily access these items. Don't just scatter them in the drawer. Use containers and organizers to hold small objects.

Credenzas and bookcases should hold materials and documents you use less frequently but need to have nearby. You can sort shelves by subject or cluster like things, such as manuals, catalogs, etc. Organize files inside the credenza and file cabinets using the labeling criteria established in this module.

Set aside a place to handle mail. You need an in-basket for incoming mail and an out-basket for documents you are sending. Do a Sort and Toss Session for your in-basket twice a day. Handle each piece of mail as quickly as possible, using the sort and toss criteria from this module.

HOW DO YOU HANDLE THESE ENVIRONMENTAL CHALLENGES?

- A work space near the coffee room with heavy traffic all day
- A work space that makes you appear to be the office receptionist
- A work space near the mail room with constant activity, deliveries, and noise
- A work space near a bank of filing cabinets used by the entire department
- A poorly ventilated work space
- A poorly lit work space
- A work space with too much furniture

Team Activity: Organizing Items

 Show Overhead 2.9: Organize These Items.

 Facilitator: Distribute Handout 2.7: Organize These Items.

> *Organize These Items*
>
> - Eliminate obsolete and duplicate documents.
> - Refer documents.
> - Create historical files.
> - Update manuals.
> - Cluster like things.
> - File loose papers or house them in a binder.
>
> 2.9

Instructions to Participants: Working with your team, decide how you will organize the items on the list using the information you learned from this module. Your goal is to:

- Identify and eliminate obsolete and duplicate documents.
- Refer documents to those with direct responsibility for them.
- Create historical files away from the main work area.
- Update manuals.
- Cluster like things such as manuals, catalogs, and books, or cluster by topics, e.g., company communications, personnel management, training.
- File loose papers or house them in a binder with tabs.

  You have fifteen minutes for this exercise.

 Facilitator: Bring the room to order and ask two to three teams to share some of their solutions. Ask for questions.

MANAGING PHONES AND EMAIL (10 MINUTES)

 Show Overhead 2.10: Managing Phones.

 Facilitator: Distribute Handout 2.8: Telephone Dos and Don'ts.

> *Managing Phones*
>
> - Cluster phone activity.
> - Make sure messages have complete information.
> - Update voicemail message daily.
> - Keep the phone area neat.
> - Avoid telephone tag.
> - Leave thorough voicemail messages.
> - Program frequently used numbers.
>
> 2.10

Commentary

Ask people what gets in the way of getting things done, and the most common answer is the telephone, quickly followed by email. But used efficiently, both of these tools can free productive time.

ORGANIZE THESE ITEMS

Item	How will you organize it?
Catalogs from office supply company for 1993, 1996, 1999, 2000	
Training manuals for three workshops: business writing, time management, and customer service	
Invoices from three vendors: office supplies, water delivery, and software products	
Company annual reports for past five years	
Brochures for upcoming workshops and seminars	
Telephone lists	
Meeting records for three projects: installation of new software, new customer service standards, and new product introduction	
Magazine articles on diversity, customer complaints, and sales tips	
Leads for new business	
Twenty-five business cards	
Invitation to a retirement dinner for a coworker	
New procedures for using company credit cards and handling incoming telephone calls	
Information about the company's health care and 401(k) plans	
Notes from three classes you recently attended: stress management, time management, and selling skills	
Information on the department's computer network	

Item	How will you organize it?
Paper clips, Post-it® Notes, staples, stapler, Liquid Paper, telephone, pictures of kids, pictures of cats, cartoon, pens, pencils, scissors, notebooks, dictionary, style manual, ruler, erasers, highlighters, desk lamp, clock, stuffed cow, ceramic cow	
Diskettes—blank and used	
Telephone directory	
List of phone usage for past three months	
Unsigned vendor contracts	

TELEPHONE DOS AND DON'TS

Dos

- Speak clearly and enunciate every word precisely.
- Speak more slowly than you would if you were meeting in person since it takes people longer to process auditory messages.
- Keep your greeting brief. Identify yourself and your reason for calling.
- Always leave your phone number. Don't make the other person look it up.
- Sound friendly and professional.
- Make friends with secretaries, administrative assistants, and receptionists.
- Ask permission before putting someone on hold, and explain why it is necessary. Thank her when you return to the phone.
- Focus your attention on the other person.
- Ask the person if this is a good time to talk.
- Plan what you want to accomplish with the call.
- Leave a message that states times when you can be reached by phone.

Don'ts

- Record long, cutesy voicemail messages or greetings that sound unprofessional.
- Put people on hold indefinitely.
- Carry on side conversations while you are on the phone.
- Allow interruptions while you are on the phone.
- Type on your computer keyboard while you are on the phone.
- Read your email while you are on the phone.
- Deliver a canned greeting.
- Persist if the person gives you a firm "no."
- Play telephone tag.
- Speed up when you leave your phone number.

It's most productive to schedule blocks of time to handle calls. Use your daily planner to set aside time each day for call work. In this way, you can prioritize calls and handle the most important or urgent ones first.

Phone messages should always include all of the following information:

- The caller's full name—correctly spelled
- The caller's telephone number with area code and time zone
- The date and time of the call
- The name of the company the caller works for
- Detailed message of what the caller wants
- A time when the caller will be available for a return call
- The message taker's name and phone number or extension

If someone takes messages for you, make sure they understand these requirements. If you use voicemail to take messages, update your greeting daily, clearly stating the date, your name, and a time when you will be at your desk to take incoming calls or when you will be available to return calls. Give callers the option of transferring to another person, if possible.

Keep pens and a message pad near the phone. Some people recommend that you keep a phone log to provide a written record of incoming and outgoing messages.

Make sure the area around the phone is clear of clutter so you can take messages without knocking things on the floor. Before making return calls, complete any needed research and have at hand papers and information necessary for the call. If you need to refer to files or documents, keep them near the phone so you don't have to search for them when you are on the phone.

To avoid "telephone tag," when you leave a message, indicate when you will be available to take a return call. Also include your name and phone number with area code so the person you are calling doesn't have to take time to look it up. Make it easy for people to call you back.

Leave thorough voicemail messages. You can effectively use voicemail to ask and answer questions, move projects along, schedule meetings, and avoid long-winded people. To avoid lengthy conversations, call just before lunch or the end of the day. If you don't want to speak directly with someone, call when you know he will be out and leave a message on voicemail.

When you are on the road, make sure someone in the office knows your schedule and where you can be reached. Give your pager and cell phone numbers only to those who need to know. We'll cover time management when you travel at the end of the workshop in Module 9: Managing Time on the Road and Course Assessment.

Program your most commonly used phone numbers into speed-dial, and keep a directory of frequently used numbers near the phone. Contact software can be used to dial phone numbers through your modem.

Show Overhead 2.11: Managing Email.

 Facilitator: Distribute Handout 2.9: Email Dos and Don'ts.

Managing Email

- Send only simple documents.
- Do not send confidential information.
- Cluster email activity.
- Screen by sender's name and subject line.
- Be concise and professional.

2.11

Commentary

Email can be a productivity booster if handled properly. Email lets you respond instantly and avoid telephone tag. It is more economical and can be more convenient than faxes and phone calls. You can send emails at any time and read them at your leisure. You can attach documents and even send scanned images electronically. But email has its drawbacks.

Email servers must translate documents, and formatting is often lost or garbled as documents are translated from one server to another. Messages can also be damaged. When sending attachments, make sure the document is saved in a format that is compatible with the recipient's software. If appearance is important, sending attachments may not be the most efficient means of transmission.

Never send confidential information via email or use email if you need a signature.

As with phone calls, set aside blocks of time to retrieve and respond to emails. Decide what to open using the sender's name and the subject line as criteria. If you don't know who sent the email or if the subject line is ambiguous, you may not want to open it because of the possibility of computer viruses. Never download files from strangers, and make sure your virus software scans all electronic messages and attachments for viruses.

When sending emails, make sure the subject line clearly describes the email contents so that the recipient knows to open it. Take time writing emails and responding to them. Keep your message concise, and save anything longer than a single screen for a snail mail letter or fax or make it an attachment to the email.

Your employer may have the right to intercept and read email messages, so keep them businesslike and don't write anything you wouldn't want published in the employee newsletter. Run the document through your spell checker before mailing it, and honor rules of grammar and punctuation. If you forward messages, be selective when you create your mailing list and only send the messages to people who need to receive them.

Ask for questions.

EMAIL DOS AND DON'TS

Dos Receiving Email

- Check email regularly.
- Establish reading priorities based on subject and sender.
- Respond promptly.
- Be polite.
- Save emails you need for documentation.

Dos Sending Email

- Prepare what you want to say ahead of time.
- Be brief.
- Use descriptive subject lines.
- Be polite.
- Tell the recipient what action you want him to take early in the email.
- When replying, check to see who is getting your reply and edit the list, if necessary.
- Save emails you need for documentation.
- Regularly delete old email.

Don'ts Sending Email

- Ramble.
- Respond if you are angry or feeling any strong emotion.
- Flame—use all caps or exclamation marks.
- Be terse or abrupt.
- Give commands.
- Assume your email will be read.
- Send confidential messages.
- Send more than one attachment with each message.

Don'ts Receiving Email

- Open or respond to emails or download files from strangers.
- Save emails unless you need them for documentation.
- Forward jokes unless you know the recipient wants them.

MANAGING COMPUTER FILES AND SOFTWARE (10 MINUTES)

 Show Overhead 2.12: Managing Computer Files and Software.

 Facilitator: Distribute Handout 2.10: Checklist for Managing Computer Files and Software.

> ### Managing Computer Files and Software
>
> - Label computer files.
> - Archive old files.
> - Label diskettes.
> - Delete obsolete files and software.
> - Back up daily.
> - Learn how to save time with software.
> - Make sure computer is positioned correctly.
> - Take regular breaks.
>
> 2.12

Commentary

Computer files should be set up and labeled using the same system you use for paper files. Label directories and subdirectories, and add documents to them just as you do for paper files.

Some people use color diskettes or diskette labels to differentiate major categories of computer files. For example, green might be used to identify financial files and blue, personnel files. If you use color coding for computer files, carry the color scheme over to your paper files.

Like paper files, you probably need to clean up your computer files. Start by viewing files according to date, and file off old files to an archive diskette. Make sure you label the diskette so you can find the files. If appropriate, delete old drafts of completed projects, working drafts of documents, and software you don't use.

Make sure you back up your files at least once daily. If appropriate, carry key files with you on diskettes.

To save time when using software:

- Create templates for frequently used documents such as invoices, standard contracts, fax cover sheets, and purchase orders. Create macros for frequently used phrases such as your company's name.

- Learn how to use software efficiently. Some software lets you take phone messages and send them directly to the person's email address. Contact software helps you organize your phone directory electronically, keep track of calls and correspondence, and remind you of appointments and the need for follow-up. You can use the merge feature to generate mass mailings that look and read like customized, personalized letters. Spreadsheet software can help you keep track of expenses, inventory, and other items that require analysis. Presentation software can add punch and pizzazz to overheads and slides.

- Use shortcuts and keyboard commands rather than the mouse.

CHECKLIST FOR MANAGING COMPUTER FILES AND SOFTWARE

❏ Set up and label computer files using the same system you use for paper files.

❏ File off old files to an archive diskette.

❏ Label diskettes so you can find files.

❏ Delete old drafts of completed projects, working drafts of documents, and, if appropriate, software you don't use.

❏ Back up your files at least once daily.

❏ If appropriate, carry key files with you on diskettes.

❏ To save time when using software:

- Create templates for frequently used documents and macros for frequently used phrases.
- Learn how to use software efficiently.
- Use shortcuts and commands.

❏ Make sure your computer is positioned for comfort and doesn't strain your vision or posture.

❏ Take a five-minute break every hour. Look away from your monitor, stand, and stretch.

Make sure your computer is positioned for comfort and doesn't strain your vision or posture. Take a five-minute break every hour. Look away from your monitor, stand, and stretch.

Ask for questions.

Break: We've covered a lot of territory this morning. We are now going to take a one-hour lunch break. During the break, if you think of any questions you want answered, jot them down and we'll discuss them when we return. Please return to the room by [time] for the next module.

GETTING ORGANIZED NOTES

Review Module 1	The three most important things you learned in Module 1:
	1.
	2.
	3.
	Three action items:
	1.
	2.
	3.
Getting Organized	
Objectives for Module 2	
Principles of Organization	

Clearing Clutter and Creating Order	Sort and Toss Session
Creating a Filing System So You Can Find Things	What to keep
	Filing strategies
Organizing the Work Space	
Managing Phones and Email	Phones
	Email
Managing Computer Files and Software	

Developing Concentration and Focus (1.5 hours)

OBJECTIVES FOR MODULE 3
- Focus energy and attention on what's important.
- Learn how to enter and use flow states for greater productivity.
- Identify, reduce, and eliminate distractions and interruptions.

MATERIALS NEEDED
- Handout 3.1: Organization Obstacles and Solutions
- Handout 3.2: Your Concentration Quotient
- Handout 3.3: Where Does Your Concentration Go?
- Handout 3.4: Controlling Your Environment
- Handout 3.5: Interruption Action Plan
- Handout 3.6: Checklist for Listening Skills
- Overhead 3.1: Developing Concentration and Focus
- Overhead 3.2: Objectives for Module 3
- Overhead 3.3: When You Pay Attention
- Overhead 3.4: Controlling Distractions

- Overhead 3.5: Handling Interruptions
- Overhead 3.6: Handling Interruptions (continued)
- Overhead 3.7: Learning to Concentrate by Listening

AGENDA

Review Module 2	15 minutes
Introduce Module 3: Developing Concentration and Focus	10 minutes
Paying Attention	15 minutes
Handling Distractions	20 minutes
Handling Interruptions	20 minutes
Using Listening Skills to Improve Concentration	10 minutes

REVIEW MODULE 2 (15 MINUTES)

 Facilitator: Welcome people back from lunch and bring the room to order.

Team Activity: Overcoming Organization Obstacles

Instructions to Participants: Before we start the next module on concentration and focus, let's review what we learned in Module 2: Getting Organized.

 Facilitator: Distribute Handout 3.1: Organization Obstacles and Solutions.

Place a check mark by the statements that apply to you. Then, working with your team, brainstorm solutions to one of the items on your list. You have fifteen minutes for this exercise.

 Facilitator: Call the room to order. Ask two to three volunteers to share their solutions.

INTRODUCE MODULE 3: DEVELOPING CONCENTRATION AND FOCUS (10 MINUTES)

 Show Overhead 3.1: Developing Concentration and Focus.

> *Developing Concentration and Focus*
>
> **3.1**

Commentary

What are you paying attention to? One thing or twenty? Are you present, in the moment, or are you worrying about tomorrow? Maybe you're chewing on a mistake you made yesterday—or ten years ago.

Productivity starts with the ability to concentrate and direct your energy and attention to the task at hand. Learning to pay attention and concentrate is key to entering flow states where work is easy and effortless. When you fail to concentrate, your attention wanders, and you dissipate your energy. You do a little bit of many—often, unimportant—things instead of a lot of a few *important* things. You spend the day feeling scattered and end it wondering where your time went. You feel dissatisfied and frustrated because you aren't getting things done.

Some people have highly developed concentration skills. Are you one of them? Can you block out almost all distractions and work anywhere—at

ORGANIZATION OBSTACLES AND SOLUTIONS

Instructions: Place a check mark by the statements that apply to you.

___ I don't have time to get organized.

___ I don't know where to begin.

___ I have a hard time finding anything on my desk.

___ I haven't filed in more than a week.

___ My in-basket is always overflowing.

___ I have stacks of papers on the floor.

___ I have unread magazines that are more than one month old.

___ I have Post-it® Notes all over my desk and computer.

___ I don't have/use a calendar system.

___ I hate to throw anything away.

___ I spend a lot of time looking for stuff.

___ I don't remember where I have filed papers.

___ No one can help me organize my stuff.

___ I have business cards everywhere.

___ Things pop out of my drawers when I open them.

___ I have a lot of equipment and/or personal items on my desk.

___ I have very little room on my desktop to work.

___ I have lots of files with very few papers in each file folder.

Choose one of the items you checked and, working with your team, brainstorm solutions to eliminate it.

airports, on subways, in train stations? Is it easy for you to return to the task at hand after being interrupted? Do you practice strategies for minimizing disruptions? If so, you are one of these lucky people who have mastered concentration and focus. This is an incredibly powerful productivity tool.

Concentration is the ability to focus on the task in front of you without allowing distractions or interruptions to sidetrack you. Have you ever been so engrossed in a movie or book that you lost track of everything else around you? That's concentration. According to experts who study concentration, your mind is both alert and relaxed when you are focused on something. It's easy to focus on something we enjoy doing. It's harder to focus on something that doesn't naturally hold our interest. But if you can learn to apply concentration to all aspects of your work, imagine how much faster you will get things done and how much more satisfaction you will feel at the end of the day. The ability to concentrate is especially important when you are on a deadline and every minute counts!

 Show Overhead 3.2: Objectives for Module 3.

Objectives for Module 3
• Focus energy and attention on what's important.
• Learn how to enter and use flow states.
• Identify, reduce, and eliminate distractions and interruptions.
3.2 © 2001 Patricia Haddock

Commentary

This module will teach you how to:

- Focus energy and attention on what's important.

- Learn how to enter and use flow states for greater productivity.

- Identify, reduce, and eliminate distractions and interruptions.

Mastering concentration will help you become more mindful. You will notice details more and appreciate the present moment. You won't miss your infant's first smile because you are thinking about the report that's due tomorrow. You won't miss the humor in the joke because you're wondering what to cook for dinner. You won't miss the subtle body language of a client because you're distracted by someone's beeper.

Concentration will put more time in your life. You will complete tasks faster and more effectively, and that will raise your self-esteem and confidence. You will appear more competent, and that will increase your credibility and influence.

Concentration can help you enter flow. Flow occurs when what you are doing appears to be effortless. You seem to move into a different dimension where time stands still. You are completely present to the moment and are in a mindful state. You don't worry about what you are doing, and you are not concerned about the results. You are lost in the moment.

When you are totally engaged in a task or activity so that you seem to drop out of time, you are in flow. It's like playing an intense game of chess or a computer game. You seem to become one with the activity to the exclusion of everything else. Time has no meaning, and hours can pass without your awareness. Everything does, indeed, flow. Work becomes effortless.

Athletes often experience flow. Did you ever see the brilliant quarterback Joe Montana step back into the pocket and stand there calmly looking for a receiver as chaos broke out all around him? He completely ignored the smashing of 300-pound men around him and scanned the field. It seemed as if he had stepped out of time. Then, he would spot a likely receiver and throw the ball. The instant the ball left his hands, the chaos overwhelmed him and he was tackled. But for one brief moment, Joe Montana was in flow. And most of the time, when he was in flow, his pass hit the mark. Again and again.

Generally, you enter flow when you are performing a task or activity that you enjoy and that challenges you. Developing your concentration skills and applying concentration to tasks and activities that challenge you can help you enter and remain in flow.

Individual Exercise: What's Your Concentration Quotient?

 Facilitator: Distribute Handout 3.2: Your Concentration Quotient.

Instructions to Participants: If you are like most people, your concentration skills are random and unfocused. Let's start by finding out how you concentrate and what you pay attention to. Take this quick assessment and find out. You have five minutes for this exercise.

Debriefing: Give yourself 4 points for every "Strongly Disagree" answer, 3 points for every "Disagree" answer, 2 points for every "Agree" answer, and 1 point for every "Strongly Disagree" answer.

If your score is 40–30, you have strongly developed concentration skills. This module can help you hone those skills in certain areas and show you how to apply those skills with greater effectiveness.

If your score is 20–29, you have developed some concentration and focus skills but may be distracted too easily. You could become more productive and effective. This module will help you deepen your skills and show you how to apply focus and attention with greater effectiveness.

If your score is less than 19, you are losing productivity. You need to strengthen your concentration skills so that you can control your time more effectively and not give it away. This module will show you how your mind works and teach you how to control attention and focus. You will learn how to apply focus, momentum, and energy to your work.

YOUR CONCENTRATION QUOTIENT

	Strongly Disagree	Disagree	Agree	Strongly Agree
People frequently interrupt me.				1
When I am interrupted, it's hard to return my attention to the task at hand.		3		1
When people interrupt me, I am reluctant to cut them off so I can go back to work.			2	1
My attention wanders frequently.				1
I find it difficult to concentrate.		3		
I often ask people to repeat what they say.				1
I daydream a lot.				1
I often feel frustrated at the end of the day because I haven't accomplished anything.			2	
I often feel scattered and ineffective.			2	
My office/cubicle makes people feel comfortable when they visit.		3		

PAYING ATTENTION (15 MINUTES)
Commentary

Take a moment and notice the quality of the light around you. The light you see is *diffused*—it is scattered fairly equally throughout the space you are in. You can read in this light, but there is no real power in it.

If you were to take this same light and focus it into a tight beam—narrower than the circumference of a pencil—you would have light so concentrated that you could cut metal with it. This is a laser—*concentrated* light.

For most people, most of the time, your concentration is like diffused light—scattered and unfocused. What happens if you take that scattered concentration and focus it? Two powerful things begin to happen that will give you more time, more energy, and more power.

 Show Overhead 3.3: When You Pay Attention.

> **When You Pay Attention**
>
> • Energy flows where attention goes.
> • Now is the moment of power.
>
> 3.3   © 2001 Famous Handbook

The first thing that happens is that energy flows where attention goes. You accomplish more, faster and more easily. If your attention is scattered, your energy is scattered. You accomplish a little of many things, instead of a lot of a few things. You feel frustrated, and that diminishes your energy even more. When you focus, however, you beam your energy onto the task in front of you, and it gets done faster and more easily than you can imagine.

The second thing that happens is that now comes the moment of power. You can think about the past and influence the future, but you can act only in the present. The present is the point of power. If you waste the present moment, you lose opportunities. Concentration keeps you in the present and puts great power at your disposal.

Mountain climbers are masters of concentration. They focus on what is directly in front of them, narrowing their attention so that they are totally focused on the present moment. Any distraction, any interruption, can jeopardize the climber's life. While you don't need to develop the concentration required to climb a mountain, you can improve your ability to concentrate in order to climb that stack of work in front of you.

Concentration is a habit. Like all habits, it can be learned. When you decide to develop your concentration, begin by becoming aware of how your mind works. William James, the father of American psychology, was once asked how long the mind can hold a single thought. He replied about four seconds. This means that fifteen times a minute, our concentration wanders.

Group Discussion

Lead a group discussion and brainstorm reasons why people don't pay attention. List the reasons on a flipchart. Some reasons are boredom, external noise, visual distractions, doing more than one thing at a time, poor communication skills on the part of the speaker, or sleepiness.

Commentary

The Zen Buddhists say we suffer from "monkey mind." Like monkeys traveling through the trees, jumping from limb to limb, our minds jump from thought to thought. We're here, there, everywhere—in the past, in the future—but rarely in the present. The good news is that you can control what you think about.

Once you understand how your mind works, you can practice concentration. One easy way to develop this skill is to practice concentrating on a single task for five minutes without distractions. This will require an effort of will and a degree of patience. When your mind wanders, gently bring it back to the task. Don't beat yourself up. The easiest way to bring yourself back to the present is to focus on your breathing. Just notice the inhalations and exhalations.

When you can concentrate in five-minute chunks, increase concentration time by five-minute increments until you can concentrate for thirty minutes. Now, add distractions. Play the radio or turn on the television to create background noise. The goal is to master concentration so you can concentrate anywhere, at any time, despite distractions.

When you notice your attention wandering, bring it back to the present moment and refocus. You might have to do this hundreds of times until you can focus for long periods of time. The more you practice being present, the more you will develop your concentration skills.

Make sure you give yourself breaks about every sixty minutes. Get up, walk around, and stretch. You will find that when your concentration skills improve, you will have to set an alarm to remind yourself to move!

You might also want to change projects or tasks every two to three hours. This can refresh your ability to pay attention because you have something new to work on. When you return to the original task, you will discover new insights and feel refreshed. Some people hop from task to task because they enjoy variety and tend to get sidetracked. If you tend to hop around, make sure you accomplish as much as you can before changing projects or tasks. Change to a different task or project as a reward for accomplishing a certain goal on the project at hand.

Give yourself more structure, and use your calendar to make sure you schedule important activities each day. If you are hopping because you are bored, you may need to talk to your manager about taking on more challenging work or a developmental assignment that lets you learn new skills. If that's not possible, set your own personal best goal and raise the bar for how productive you can be each day.

Individual Exercise: Where Does Your Concentration Go?

 Facilitator: Distribute Handout 3.3: Where Does Your Concentration Go?

Instructions to Participants: Where does your concentration go? For the next two minutes, list everything you notice around you. What do you see? Hear? Touch or feel? Taste or smell? Note everything without stopping for two minutes.

 Facilitator: Call the room to order.

Debriefing: Go around the room and call on participants to read what they noted.

Break: Take a five-minute stretch break.

HANDLING DISTRACTIONS (20 MINUTES)

 Show Overhead 3.4: Controlling Distractions.

Commentary

If you're like most people who do this exercise, you notice many things in your environment. Interestingly, most people discover elements in their environment they never noticed before! Notice which list has the

> *Controlling Distractions*
>
> • Visual
> • Auditory
> • Kinesthetic
>
> _____
> 3.4   © 2001 Patricia Haddock

most items: sight, hearing, touch or feel, or smell/taste. Most people have a dominant sense that they use to experience the world. People who rely on sight are called "visual." People who use hearing are "auditory." Touch, taste, and smell fall in the "kinesthetic" category. Is your dominant sense sight or hearing? These are the most common, followed by touch. Taste and smell are last.

Your dominant sense may be your greatest source of distractions. For example, if sight is dominant, you are probably most susceptible to visual distractions. If this is the case, positioning your desk by a window may not be a good idea.

If hearing is your dominant sense, you need an environment that is quiet since sound will distract you.

WHERE DOES YOUR CONCENTRATION GO?

Instructions: Where does your concentration go? For the next two minutes, list everything you notice around you. What do you see? Hear? Touch or feel? Taste or smell? Note everything without stopping for two minutes.

Sight	Hearing
Touch or Feel	**Smell/Taste**

List here three steps you will take to make your work environment less distracting:

1. _____

2. _____

3. _____

If touch or feel is your dominant sense, you need to create an environment that makes you feel safe and is conducive to concentration. For example, you may be distracted and unable to concentrate if the room temperature isn't just right or the area doesn't "feel right."

When you know where distractions are likely to come from, you can take steps to reduce their impact or eliminate them. The key to success is to do what works for you and not judge yourself.

You have to train yourself not to give in to distractions. Refuse to be side-tracked by friendly coworkers or ringing phones. Some distractions come in the form of worry. If you tend to be a worrier, set aside "worry time" each day. If your concentration wanders into worry during the day, remind yourself that you have worry time scheduled, and firmly return your attention to the work at hand.

Your environment can contribute to your ability to concentrate—or it can add to the distractions that prevent you from concentrating. Some people enjoy distractions, especially if they are working on something that bores them. If you find yourself looking for distractions because you are bored, give yourself permission to indulge in a distracting activity after a certain amount of work as a reward.

Team Activity: Controlling Your Environment

 Facilitator: Distribute Handout 3.4: Controlling Your Environment.

Instructions to Participants: Identify the environmental obstacles that prevent you from developing concentration and focus. Work with your team to come up with at least one strategy for eliminating or reducing the negative impact of this obstacle. You have ten minutes for this exercise.

 Facilitator: Call the room to order and ask for two to three volunteers to share their obstacles and solutions.

CONTROLLING YOUR ENVIRONMENT

Instructions: Identify the environmental obstacles that prevent you from developing concentration and focus. Work with your team to come up with one strategy for eliminating or reducing the negative impact of this obstacle. You have ten minutes for this exercise.

- Inadequate lighting
- Uncomfortable chair and/or desk
- Clutter
- Noisy neighbors and/or equipment
- Ringing phones
- Visitors
- Being situated in a high-traffic area
- Background noise
- Poor airflow
- Temperature too hot/too cold
- Other:

HANDLING INTERRUPTIONS (20 MINUTES)

Commentary

No matter how good your concentration skills, unless you are a hermit in a cave, people will interrupt you. The phone will ring. Someone or something will demand your attention. How do you currently handle interruptions?

Group Discussion

Lead a group discussion and have participants share the strategies they currently use to handle interruptions, such as removing visitor chairs from offices and cubicles, standing when meeting visitors, using key phrases to end conversations.

 Show Overhead 3.5: Handling Interruptions.

If you don't handle interruptions well or want some new ideas for handling them, here are some tips to help you:

> *Handling Interruptions*
>
> * Allow time in schedule.
> * Identify patterns.
> * Be assertive.
> * Use wrap-up phrases.
> * Handle phones.
> * Schedule undisturbed time.
>
> 3.5   © 2001 Patricia Haddock

- Allow time in your schedule to handle interruptions. If you schedule your day too tightly or rigidly, you won't be able to make up time lost to interruptions.

- Who interrupts you and when? Keep a time log for a few days or a week. Do you see a pattern? Is the same person asking the same questions? A call from a friend coming at the same time each day? Eliminate the interruption before it occurs. Consider additional training for the employee who asks too many questions. Call your friend at night and refuse to take his call during the day.

- Tell people when you are on a deadline, and refuse to let them disturb you unless you are ready to take a break anyway.

- Use "wrap-up" phrases, such as "Let's wrap this up," "If there is nothing more, let's wrap it up now," and "We'll have to continue this later."

- Make sure you have an organized system to handle telephone calls. Review your notes and handouts from Module 2: Getting Organized.

- Schedule time on your calendar when you will not be disturbed. If someone tries to interrupt you, politely explain that you are in the middle of something and can't give her your attention right now.

Show Overhead 3.6: Handling Interruptions (continued).

> *Handling Interruptions (continued)*
>
> * Be unavailable.
> * Leave the office.
> * Postpone routine matters.
> * Use email and voicemail.
> * Don't socialize.
> * Politely ask visitors to leave.
> * Don't interrupt others.
> * Learn to concentrate.
>
> **3.6**

* Close your door, or leave your cubicle and go to an empty office or conference room.
* Get out of the office entirely. If you're able, take your laptop to the local coffee shop or a park bench. Telecommute, but don't let your family interrupt you with errands and demands for attention.
* Ask people to postpone routine matters. Set aside time each day for dealing with routine matters, and encourage people to meet with you during that time. Make sure everyone knows when your door is open and you are receptive to interruptions.
* Encourage people to use email and voicemail so you can respond at your convenience.
* Stop answering the phone for part of each day. Let voicemail or the receptionist take messages. If you must answer the phone, immediately find out if you can return the call later in the day. End the call as soon as possible.
* Don't encourage socializing. Remove visitors' chairs from your office or cubicle. Turn your desk so you don't face the door.
* When someone just drops in, immediately stand and remain standing. Either ask him to return later, at a specific time, or tell him you can spare only five minutes. When the five minutes are up, ask him to leave and promise to call him later. Make sure you follow up.
* Don't be an interruption for others.
* Use interruptions to train yourself to concentrate. Immediately return to the task you were doing and focus, focus, focus.

As with distractions, some people like to be interrupted. Worse, they are an interruption for others. If this describes you, it is important that you take control of this tendency and consciously plan when and how you will be interrupted. Resist the urge to interrupt others.

Individual Exercise: Identifying and Eliminating Interruptions

 Facilitator: Distribute Handout 3.5: Interruption Action Plan.

Instructions to Participants: Working alone, identify the most common interruptions you must cope with, and decide how you will handle them in the

INTERRUPTION ACTION PLAN

Instructions: The Boy Scout motto, "Be prepared," is good advice. Don't wait until you are trying to finish a report on deadline to figure out how you are going to handle interruptions. Start now to identify, reduce, and eliminate sources of interruptions.

The most common interruptions I cope with are:

_____

_____

_____

I will implement the following strategies for eliminating these interruptions in the future:

_____

_____

_____

future, using the strategies from this module. Then share one of your strategies with your team. You have fifteen minutes for this exercise.

USING LISTENING SKILLS TO IMPROVE CONCENTRATION (10 MINUTES)
Commentary

While it is important to control interruptions, it is also necessary to develop strong interpersonal relationships at work. We need to work with others to get things done, and we don't want to develop a reputation for being aloof.

When people are deeply concentrating, they may appear to be abrupt and rude and seem to ignore others. If you concentrate easily and well, you may want to watch your "people" skills to find out if you're being viewed as aloof or rude. If so, pay more attention to the people factor, and take others' feelings into account. This may mean spending a few minutes visiting around the water cooler, chatting with someone in your office a few minutes longer than usual, or seeking out other people. Take control of downtime so that it doesn't interrupt your concentration or disrupt your day.

 Show Overhead 3.7: Learning to Concentrate by Listening.

Learning to Concentrate by Listening

3.7

Listening is one of the most important interpersonal skills you can master. Conflicts and problems arise because we don't hear each other. We think people have said something when, in fact, they haven't. A good listener reduces mistakes and misunderstandings that can cost time, money, and harmony.

Listening is also one of the best ways to hone your concentration skills because effective listening requires intense concentration. Remember: You can only hold a single thought for about four seconds, so your mind will wander when someone is speaking, especially if she is droning.

 Facilitator: Distribute Handout 3.6: Checklist for Listening Skills.

Active listening requires you to pay attention to what the other person is saying *as it is being said*. It requires you to be totally present and to focus on the other person. If your attention wanders, gently bring it back. These are the things you need to do:

- Let people finish speaking before responding. Don't try to formulate a response while someone else is speaking because you may miss important information.

CHECKLIST FOR LISTENING SKILLS

❏ Let people finish speaking before responding.

❏ Stay present.

❏ Demonstrate that you are paying attention.

❏ Pay attention to body language.

❏ Establish rapport.

❏ Control the conversation.

❏ Concentrate on facts and behaviors.

❏ Use silence.

- Stay present.

- Demonstrate that you are paying attention. You can do this in a variety of ways. Smile, nod, maintain eye contact, and use encouraging phrases such as "Go ahead . . . I see . . . ."

- Pay attention to body language. The body can speak louder than words. A defensive body language belies the person who says nothing is wrong. Observe how the other person uses his or her body to better understand what's going on beneath the surface.

- Establish rapport. An easy way to make someone feel comfortable is to subtly mirror his body language. If the other person sits forward with both elbows on the desk, try sitting slightly forward with your elbows on the chair arms. Also, paraphrase what you think you heard, and ask if your interpretation is correct. Repeat the key phrases and words the person uses.

- Control the conversation. To expand a conversation, use open-ended questions that encourage responses. Open-ended questions that begin with "what" and "how" require more than a "yes" or "no" answer. Other open-ended questions are "Can you tell me a little more about that?" and "What's your opinion about this?" To limit a conversation, ask closed-ended questions that elicit only "yes" or "no" answers.

- Concentrate on facts and behaviors. Require straightforward answers to your questions by rephrasing them until the person responds.

- Silence can be a powerful form of communication, and you can use silence to draw out a response from a reluctant speaker. Allow silences to descend on a conversation, and learn to feel comfortable without speaking.

Developing concentration and focus is a critical skill that can increase your productivity and effectiveness on and off the job. Work on honing your concentration skills every day, and soon you will be speeding through tasks.

Ask for questions.

Break: We're going to take a fifteen-minute break. Please return promptly at [time].

Developing Concentration and Focus—Notes

Review Module 2	
Introduce Module 3: Developing Concentration and Focus	
Paying Attention	
Handling Distractions	
Handling Interruptions	
Using Listening Skills to Improve Concentration	

Making Friends with Procrastination (2 Hours)

OBJECTIVES FOR MODULE 4

- Understand and recognize the factors that contribute to procrastination.
- Learn strategies for working with procrastination.

MATERIALS NEEDED

- Handout 4.1: Eliminating Workplace Distractions
- Handout 4.2: What Is Your Procrastination Pattern?
- Handout 4.3: Remembering Your Past Successes
- Handout 4.4: What Does Success Mean to You?
- Handout 4.5: Steps for Effective Delegation
- Handout 4.6: Avoiding Procrastination in the Future
- Overhead 4.1: Making Friends with Procrastination
- Overhead 4.2: Objectives for Module 4
- Overhead 4.3: Factors Contributing to Procrastination
- Overhead 4.4: Fear and Procrastination
- Overhead 4.5: Being Overwhelmed and Procrastination

- Overhead 4.6: Setting Priorities
- Overhead 4.7: Perfectionism and Procrastination
- Overhead 4.8: Distaste and Procrastination
- Overhead 4.9: Steps for Effective Delegation
- Overhead 4.10: Avoiding Procrastination in the Future

AGENDA

Review Module 3	15 minutes
Making Friends with Procrastination	5 minutes
Objectives for Module 4	20 minutes
Fear and Procrastination	30 minutes
Being Overwhelmed and Procrastination	15 minutes
Perfectionism and Procrastination	5 minutes
Distaste and Procrastination	10 minutes
Avoiding Procrastination in the Future	20 minutes

REVIEW MODULE 3 (15 MINUTES)

 Facilitator: Welcome people back from lunch and bring the room to order.

Team Activity: Eliminating Workplace Distractions

 Facilitator: Refer to Handout 3.3: Where Does Your Concentration Go? Distribute Handout 4.1: Eliminating Workplace Distractions.

Instructions to Participants: Before we start the next module, let's review what we learned in Module 3: Developing Concentration and Focus. Review your answers to the "Where Does Your Concentration Go?" exercise. This exercise tells you where distractions are most likely to come from for you—visual, auditory, or kinesthetic. Work with your team so that each of you develops one strategy you can implement to help you eliminate or reduce one distraction. For example, if most of your distractions are visual and your desk faces a window, you may want to turn it so that it faces a wall. Or if you are auditory and your phone distracts you, you may want to turn off the ringer for part of each day so you can concentrate on important activities. You have fifteen minutes for this exercise.

Ask for questions.

 Facilitator: Bring the room to order and ask two to three participants to share their solutions.

INTRODUCE MODULE 4: MAKING FRIENDS WITH PROCRASTINATION (5 MINUTES)

 Show Overhead 4.1: Making Friends with Procrastination.

Making Friends with Procrastination
4.1

Commentary

You have set goals. You have identified what's most important and created a plan. You know what you have to do to get organized. You've discovered where distractions are most likely to come from, and you know how to handle interruptions. Not a bad day's work so far.

ELIMINATING WORKPLACE DISTRACTIONS

Instructions: Review your answers to the exercise from Handout 3.3: Where Does Your Concentration Go? This exercise tells you where distractions are most likely to come from for you—whether they are visual, auditory, or kinesthetic. Work with your team to develop one strategy you can implement to help you eliminate or reduce this type of distraction. For example, if most of your distractions are visual and your desk faces a window, you may want to turn it so that it faces a wall. Or if you are auditory and your phone distracts you, you may want to turn off the ringer for part of each day so you can concentrate on important activity. You have fifteen minutes for this exercise.

_____

_____

_____

_____

_____

_____

Now, when you return to your desk, you have to take action. Some of you will and some of you won't. Most of you will probably procrastinate in one or more areas. Some people are more productive and thrive when they are under the pressure of a deadline, so they procrastinate until the pressure of meeting the deadline is "just right." *Then,* they act.

Just about everyone suffers from procrastination. When we procrastinate, we do less important tasks instead of more important ones. We avoid activities we should perform and need to perform and spend our time on activities that someone else could easily do for us. Occasional procrastination usually isn't a major problem, unless it causes you to miss an important deadline or it negatively impacts your professional reputation.

Some people procrastinate all the time. Do you find yourself up all night to meet a deadline, even though you had weeks to prepare? Does your stack of filing grow taller by the minute, even though you know life would be easier if you filed all that stuff away? Are you avoiding starting a big project and working on other less important tasks instead? If so, you're procrastinating, and it is negatively affecting your reputation. People will begin to think that you are unreliable. Not only will it affect your reputation—it can affect your health. Procrastination contributes to stress and feelings of anxiety, frustration, and inadequacy. It is one of the main challenges to productivity and effective time management.

Procrastination, like pain, is a symptom. And as with pain, once we understand the reasons behind it, we can take action to end it. Procrastination can range from mild reluctance to outright loathing because we don't want to do something. When we discover why we don't want to do it, we can implement strategies for getting past the procrastination. We can take action. Procrastination gives us an opportunity to face and overcome situations and habits that detract from our productivity and effectiveness.

OBJECTIVES FOR MODULE 4 (20 MINUTES)

 Show Overhead 4.2: Objectives for Module 4.

Commentary

In this module, we will learn how to:

- Understand and recognize the factors that contribute to procrastination.

- Create strategies for working with procrastination, not fighting against it.

> *Objectives for Module 4*
>
> - Understand and recognize contributing factors.
> - Create strategies for working with procrastination.
>
> 4.2   © 2021 Patricia Haddock

Individual Exercise: Identifying Your Procrastination Pattern

 Facilitator: Distribute Handout 4.2: What Is Your Procrastination Pattern?

Instructions to Participants: Working alone, take the assessment on Handout 4.2. In Column 1, describe the situations or activities where you procrastinate. Then, in Column 2, identify why you procrastinate. You can use the list on the handout or add your own reasons if they are not on the list. You have fifteen minutes for this exercise.

Ask for questions.

 Facilitator: Bring the room to order.

 Show Overhead 4.3: Factors Contributing to Procrastination.

Commentary

Many factors contribute to procrastination. The most common are:

- Fear
- Being overwhelmed
- Perfectionism
- Distaste

We'll look at each of these and learn strategies for working with them. Let's start with fear.

Ask for questions.

Factors Contributing to Procrastination

- Fear
- Being overwhelmed
- Perfectionism
- Distaste

4.3   © 2001 Patricia Haddock

FEAR AND PROCRASTINATION (30 MINUTES)

 Show Overhead 4.4: Fear and Procrastination.

Group Discussion

Why would someone be afraid to do something? How does fear contribute to procrastination? What are some of the things that people are afraid of that would cause them to procrastinate?

Fear and Procrastination

- Success breeds success.
- Assess likelihood of worst case.
- Use goals for motivation.
- Rehearse.
- Find role models.

4.4   © 2001 Patricia Haddock

WHAT IS YOUR PROCRASTINATION PATTERN?

Instructions: What situations cause you to procrastinate? In Column 1, describe the situations or activities where you procrastinate. Then, in Column 2, identify why you are procrastinating. You can use the list on this handout, or add your own reasons if they are not on the list.

Some reasons for procrastinating:

- Anxiety
- Boredom
- Fear of failure
- Fear of success
- Feelings of inadequacy
- Inexperience
- Lack of information
- Lack of interest
- Lack of organization
- Lack of relevance
- Lack of time
- Lack of training
- Not knowing where to start
- Perfectionism
- Performance fear
- Stress
- Other:

Situation Causing Procrastination	Why You Are Procrastinating
EXAMPLE: *Learning new skills*	*Fear of failure*

Lead a group discussion about how fear can cause people to procrastinate. Fear often arises when we have to do something new or move out of our comfort zone. When this happens, we may remember events from our past when we failed to perform as well as we wanted, when we were rejected, when we were criticized by someone important to us. All of these negative memories deepen our fear of trying and compound procrastination.

Commentary

Fear can keep you from achieving what you want. It can stop you in your tracks. When you are procrastinating because you are afraid to move ahead, you need to step back and look at several factors: your past achievements, the facts about the present situation, and what motivates you.

Instead of remembering past failures or painful negative experiences, we need to remember positive things. We all have examples of past situations where we overcame our fear and did what we had to do—when we were successful. These past positive memories can help move us through procrastination.

Success breeds success. Remembering past achievements and times that you overcame obstacles can boost your confidence, give you a model to follow, and help you overcome fear.

Individual Exercise: Remembering Obstacles You Overcame

 Facilitator: Distribute Handout 4.3: Remembering Your Past Successes.

Instructions to Participants: Working alone, list three obstacles from your past that you overcame. Your list can include more than just business endeavors. State how you overcame your fear, and include the strengths you drew upon to help you succeed. You have ten minutes for this exercise.

Ask for questions.

 Facilitator: Bring the room to order. Ask two to three people to share their experiences.

Commentary

Sometimes, you are afraid because you cannot find a solution to a problem and you visualize worst-case scenarios. Do you imagine your family turning away from you if you fail? Do you see your request for a promotion or raise rejected by your boss? Do you see your job being eliminated? Knowledge can calm these fears.

Honestly assess the likelihood of the worst case happening using a scale from 5 to 1, with 5 being "100 percent certain the worst case will happen" and 1 being "100 percent certain it will never happen." Create strategies for avoiding

REMEMBERING YOUR PAST SUCCESSES

Instructions: List three obstacles from your past that you overcame. Your list can include more than just business endeavors. The more varied your list, the more you can draw on when you are procrastinating because of fear. State how you overcame your fear and include the strengths you drew upon to help you succeed.

Describe the obstacle you overcame	Describe how you overcame your fear
1.	1.
2.	2.
3.	3.

Refer to your list often and allow yourself to feel competent, accomplished, and successful as you review each achievement. Keep it handy for the tough times.

the worst case from happening by identifying actions you can take to ameliorate the situation. For example, if getting fired is a worst case, you can decide how you can avoid this by taking action now. You could let your manager know there is a problem, update your resume, or you can decide how to appropriately defend yourself. Keep in mind the worst case rarely happens. Get the information you need to reduce the likelihood of the worst case occurring. Objectively evaluate possible outcomes, and then act.

Ask for questions.

When fear prevents you from taking action, your goals can get you moving again. What does success mean to you? For many people, it means they can have more of what is important to them.

Individual Exercise: Using Goals for Motivation

 Facilitator: Distribute Handout 4.4: What Does Success Mean to You? Refer participants to Handout 1.4: Doing What's Most Important, Handout 1.5: Setting SMART Goals, and Handout 1.6: Planning to Reach Your Goals.

Instructions to Participants: Review the goals you set in Module 1: Time Management and Productivity. Working alone, identify what achieving your goals means to you. Check all that apply to you on Handout 4.4 and add any that are not on the list. You have ten minutes for this exercise.

Ask for questions.

 Facilitator: Bring the room to order.

Commentary

If you are afraid because you need to perform, rehearse what you need to do. You can practice cold calling, a speech or presentation, a job interview—just about anything that involves performance. Start with a mental rehearsal, imagining what you will do over and over until it seems natural to you. You can evaluate how you say something or how you move using just your imagination. After mentally rehearsing a few times, do a walk-through in front of a mirror. Then, ask someone you trust to evaluate your efforts and give you feedback for improving.

Read biographies and autobiographies of people who overcame their fears and succeeded. Helen Keller was deaf and blind, yet she obtained a degree from Radcliffe and became a best-selling author and lecturer.

Don't look for only famous people. People you know have all faced their fears and overcome obstacles. Talk to people you trust—a coach, mentor, friend—and find out how they did it.

Ask for questions.

WHAT DOES SUCCESS MEAN TO YOU?

Instructions: Refer to Handout 1.4: Doing What's Most Important, Handout 1.5: Setting SMART Goals, and Handout 1.6: Planning to Reach Your Goals. Review the goals you set in Module 1. Working alone, identify what achieving your goals means to you. Check all that apply to you.

By reaching my goals, I can:

___ Have more freedom.

___ Be more creative.

___ Make more money.

___ Have more fun.

___ Do what's important to me.

___ Make a contribution.

___ Get a promotion.

___ Live my bliss.

___ Have more time for _____(fill in).

___ Other: _____

BEING OVERWHELMED AND PROCRASTINATION
(15 MINUTES)

Show Overhead 4.5: Being Overwhelmed and Procrastination.

> *Being Overwhelmed and Procrastination*
>
> • You have too much to do.
> • You are facing a large, complex project.
>
> ──────────────
> 4.5   © 2001 Patricia Haddock

Commentary

Being overwhelmed is common in offices today because everyone is working harder than ever before. Many people are doing the work of two people because of downsizing.

You can feel overwhelmed because:

• You have too much to do.

• You are facing a large, complex project.

Either of these can cause procrastination. Let's look at strategies for each.

When you have too much to do, there are several steps you can take to help move forward.

• Review your goals with regard to what you need to do. Are they in sync? Are there conflicts? Do you need to revise your goals to support the additional tasks you must achieve?

• Reevaluate your priorities by asking the following questions:

Show Overhead 4.6: Setting Priorities.

> *Setting Priorities*
>
> • Does the activity contribute to goals?
> • Who values this activity? How important is this person?
> • What are the consequences of not doing it?
> • Is there a deadline?
> • Is the deadline within the next five working days?
>
> ──────────────
> 4.6   © 2001 Patricia Haddock

• Does this activity contribute to my goals?
• To whom does this activity have value, and how important is this person in my life?
• What are the consequences of not doing this activity?
• Does this activity have a deadline? If so, schedule time on your calendar to accomplish it on time.
• Is the deadline within the next five working days? If so, the activity is urgent. Rearrange your weekly plan to get it done.

- Are you clear about what is expected of you and how your performance will be measured? The clearer your understanding, the easier it will be to determine the amount of effort required.

- Is there a simpler, easier way of doing this? The scope of the task may be less than you initially think it is.

- If the additional responsibilities will adversely affect your ability to achieve your goals, you have to discuss the situation with your manager and negotiate some changes in either the scope of your job or project deadlines, or both.

- You may need to add staff—either permanent or temporary personnel.

Sometimes we have too much to do because we don't say "no" often enough. We take on many things we don't *have* to agree to do. If you are overwhelmed because you have overcommitted yourself, learn to say "no" to tasks and requests that are not directly related to your major goals. Don't just burst out "no." Explain your priorities and ask your manager to explain his or her priorities. Sometimes managers need to help you determine priorities since they should have a more global view of department activities. Your manager also needs to understand when you have conflicting priorities.

Ask for questions.

Question: How do you eat an elephant? Encourage answers from the group. Answer: One bite at a time.

You do the same when you are faced with large, complex projects. Break them down into smaller and smaller tasks with discrete deadlines that you can more easily plan to achieve. Once you identify smaller, manageable tasks, you take action one task at a time. This strategy also gives you the advantage of seeing progress early in the process. Since success adds to success, this is a good solution when you are procrastinating due to being overwhelmed.

Sometimes, you may be procrastinating because you don't know where to start. This is one of the easier procrastinators to solve. Start anywhere. Many things don't have to be done in a logical order from start to finish. Some authors start a book manuscript by writing the middle of the book first; some even write the last chapter first.

You can also schedule time every day to work on the task you are avoiding. It can be easier to get started if you know you have to work on it for only thirty minutes or an hour and then can quit for the day. Make sure you actually devote the time you set aside to the task.

Ask for questions.

PERFECTIONISM AND PROCRASTINATION (5 MINUTES)

 Show Overhead 4.7: Perfectionism and Procrastination.

> *Perfectionism and Procrastination*
>
> - Strive for accuracy, not perfection.
> - Set small, easy-to-achieve goals.
> - Use realistic standards.
> - Forgive mistakes.
> - Remember: "Good enough" is good enough.
>
> 4.7   © 2001 Patricia Haddock

Commentary

Sometimes, perfectionism leads to procrastination. We are so afraid of making a mistake, of not producing something perfectly, that we don't do anything. Perfectionism can be paralyzing.

Perfectionists value every task equally and have difficulty allocating their time based on the relative importance of each task. If you suffer from perfectionism, you need to clearly prioritize goals so you have criteria against which you can measure your efforts. Your greatest efforts should be reserved for your most important goals. Not every task or project needs the amount of time it would take to make it "perfect." In fact, the more time you devote to performing less important activities perfectly, the less time you have for more important activities.

Look at your goals. Are they realistic? You need goals that help you stretch and grow, but they must be achievable goals. Break down goals into small, easy-to-achieve steps. Remember, one hundred small steps toward your goals can take you farther than one large step—and they are easier to take.

Perfectionists also need to accept the fact that things will never be perfect. Things need to be accurate, but accuracy and perfection are not the same. If you are procrastinating because of perfectionism, you need to reevaluate your standards and make sure they are achievable.

Be gentle with yourself and forgiving of errors and mistakes. Give yourself permission to do your best the first time around with the knowledge that you can improve later. But recognize that it's important to limit the number of times you revisit it to make it "better."

Realize that "good enough" is a good enough standard for much of what we do—especially those activities that are not central to our major goals. There really isn't much difference between 98 percent and 100 percent. Multimillion-dollar baseball players are considered heroes if they hit three out of every ten pitches!

Ask for questions.

DISTASTE AND PROCRASTINATION (10 MINUTES)

 Show Overhead 4.8: Distaste and Procrastination.

Group Discussion

Sometimes, we just don't want to do something because it's an activity we don't enjoy or it is one that bores us.

Lead a discussion of reasons why people don't want to do something.

Distaste and Procrastination

- Just do it.
- Delegate it.
- Swap.
- Don't do it.
- Postpone doing it.

4.8 © 2001 Patricia Haddock.

Commentary

There are basically four strategies when we are procrastinating because we just don't want to do something.

Some things just have to be done, and whether we like it or not, they have to be done by us. We have to go to the dentist and doctor for routine exams to keep us healthy. We have to file and pay taxes. We have to talk to a team member about his negative attitude because it is adversely affecting team morale.

In these cases where we have to do things we don't want to do, it's best to make an appointment with yourself, set aside time on your calendar to get it done, and just do it. Tackle a little bit of the task each day, and make sure you give yourself a reward for finishing it. It is best if you target the most unpleasant thing first and get it out of the way. Once it is done, procrastination may disappear.

Is there any way you can make the task more pleasurable? Can you work on the budget at a local coffee house? Review the draft of your report sitting on a park bench? Plan your presentation in your favorite gallery at the museum? Whenever possible, make work fun, not work.

 Facilitator: Distribute Handout 4.5: Steps for Effective Delegation.

 Show Overhead 4.9: Steps for Effective Delegation.

Steps for Effective Delegation

1. Identify tasks that can be delegated.
2. Select the person.
3. Does he or she have the needed expertise?
4. Meet with the person to discuss the assignment.
5. Periodically obtain feedback.
6. Review results and evaluate how they measure up to expected results. Give the employee credit for a job well done.

4.9 © 2001 Patricia Haddock.

Commentary

Don't assume that you have to do something you don't like. It may make sense to delegate the task. Delegation is a good way to develop

STEPS FOR EFFECTIVE DELEGATION

1. Identify tasks that can be delegated. Spend time on activities that only you can perform—activities that require your skills and knowledge and that contribute most to the achievement of your goals. Delegate tasks that require specialized skills to those with appropriate expertise.

2. Carefully select the person to whom you will delegate the task. Match tasks with skills while giving people the opportunity to stretch and grow.

3. Ask yourself if the employee has the expertise to succeed and if he can take on this assignment and meet your deadline.

4. Meet with the employee to discuss the assignment. Explain the nature of the assignment and what results you expect. Define any limits you want recognized, encourage questions, and give feedback. Make sure the employee understands how the task contributes to the success of your department/company.

5. Periodically obtain feedback from the employee. Provide coaching, if needed, but give people autonomy.

6. Review results and evaluate how they measure up to expected results. Give the employee credit for a job well done.

employees' skills and competencies. Here are steps to follow for effective delegation:

1. Identify tasks that can be delegated. Spend time on activities that only you can perform—activities that require your skills and knowledge and that contribute most to the achievement of your goals. Often, routine tasks, such as maintaining and routing to-read folders, and recurring activities, such as status reports, can easily be delegated. Consider delegating tasks that require specialized skills to those with appropriate expertise.

2. Carefully select the person to whom you will delegate the task. Match tasks with skills while giving people the opportunity to stretch and grow.

3. Ask yourself if the employee has the expertise to succeed and if she can take on this assignment and meet your deadline.

4. Meet with the employee to discuss the assignment. Explain the nature of the assignment and what results you expect. Define any limits you want recognized, encourage questions, and give feedback. Make sure the employee understands how the task contributes to the success of your department/company.

5. Periodically obtain feedback from the employee. Provide coaching, if needed, but give people autonomy.

6. Review results and evaluate how they measure up to expected results. Give the employee credit for a job well done.

Ask for questions.

Commentary

The third strategy you can employ when you don't want to do something is to swap tasks. For example, if you hate house cleaning but love gardening and your neighbor hates gardening and doesn't mind house cleaning, you can swap tasks. You do the gardening for both of you, and your neighbor does the house cleaning.

The last strategy is to not do it. Evaluate the consequences of not doing it, and if the ramifications are not significant, just don't do it. If you decide to use this strategy, don't beat yourself up for not doing it. Let it go and move on to something else.

A variation on this strategy is to make a conscious decision to postpone doing it. In this case, make sure you create a note on your tickler system to return to this task at a later date. If you decide to postpone it, forget about it until the designated time for working on it arrives.

Ask for questions.

AVOIDING PROCRASTINATION IN THE FUTURE (20 MINUTES)
Commentary

Now that you better understand why procrastination occurs and you have strategies for dealing with it, you can stop fighting procrastination and start working with it to get things done. One of the best strategies, however, is to avoid procrastination in the first place.

 Facilitator: Distribute Handout 4.6: Avoiding Procrastination in the Future. Refer participants to Handout 4.2: What Is Your Procrastination Pattern?

This checklist for avoiding procrastination in the future shows some strategies you can employ to avoid procrastination in the future. You can add other strategies of your own.

 Show Overhead 4.10: Avoiding Procrastination in the Future.

 Facilitator: Call on one or more participants to read the list on Handout 4.6.

> *Avoiding Procrastination in the Future*
>
> - Visualize the result.
> - What are the benefits of doing it?
> - What happens if you don't do it?
> - Clear the clutter.
> - Get information.
> - Get help.
> - Set small goals.
> - Reward yourself.
>
> 4.10

Team Activity: Strategies for Avoiding Procrastination

Instructions to Participants: For the next fifteen minutes, work with your team to develop strategies for avoiding procrastination in the future using the situations and factors you identified on Handout 4.2: What Is Your Procrastination Pattern? For example, if you procrastinate when you face large projects, one strategy is to set small, easily achieved goals that you can work on for a set time each day.

Ask for questions.

Debriefing: Call the room to order and, based on the time available, ask for participants to share their strategies with the entire group.

Commentary

This concludes the first day of our workshop. We will reconvene tomorrow morning at [time]. We'll begin tomorrow with a recap of today's topics, and we'll have a question-and-answer session. Please review the time management challenges you identified at the beginning of today's sessions, which are posted around the room. Take some time to think about how you will implement what you learned today to solve these challenges and become more productive and efficient when you return to your job. We'll share some of your ideas when we meet tomorrow.

AVOIDING PROCRASTINATION IN THE FUTURE

This checklist shows some strategies you can employ to avoid procrastination in the future. You can add other strategies of your own.

❑ Visualize the result to the action steps you need to take.

❑ Write out the benefits of doing it.

❑ Write out what will happen if you don't do it or miss the deadline.

❑ Clear away clutter.

❑ Get the information you need.

❑ Get help if you need it.

❑ Set small, easily achieved goals.

❑ Reward yourself.

Work with your team to develop strategies for avoiding procrastination in the future using the situations and factors you identified in Handout 4.2: What Is Your Procrastination Pattern? For example, if you procrastinate when you face large projects, one strategy is to set small, easily achieved goals that you can work on for a set time each day.

Making Friends with Procrastination—Notes

Review Module 3	Eliminate distractions
Making Friends with Procrastination	What is procrastination?
Objectives for Module 4	What factors contribute to procrastination?
Fear and Procrastination	Strategies for overcoming procrastination due to fear
Being Overwhelmed and Procrastination	Strategies for overcoming procrastination due to being overwhelmed
Perfectionism and Procrastination	Strategies for overcoming procrastination due to perfectionism
Distaste and Procrastination	Strategies for overcoming procrastination due to distaste
Avoiding Procrastination in the Future	Strategies for avoiding procrastination in the future

PART III

DAY TWO

Understanding Work Styles (1.25 hours)

OBJECTIVES FOR MODULE 5

- Learn how to work with people who have different work styles.
- Understand how energy patterns affect productivity and how to schedule tasks accordingly.
- Understand what motivates others to take action and how to communicate with others to get things done.

MATERIALS NEEDED

- Handout 5.1: Solving Productivity Challenges
- Handout 5.2: Checklist for Larks and Owls
- Handout 5.3: What's Your Motivation Style?
- Handout 5.4: Working with Other People
- Overhead 5.1: Solving Productivity Challenges
- Overhead 5.2: Understanding Work Styles
- Overhead 5.3: Objectives for Module 5
- Overhead 5.4: Larks and Owls
- Overhead 5.5: Motivation Styles
- Overhead 5.6: Work Styles

AGENDA

Review Day One   25 minutes

Introduce Module 5   2 minutes

Objectives for Module 5   3 minutes

Energy Patterns   15 minutes

Motivation Styles   15 minutes

Working with Other People   15 minutes

REVIEW DAY ONE (25 MINUTES)

 Facilitator: Welcome people and have them break into their teams.

Commentary

Before we start on today's modules, let's review what we covered yesterday. We began the day by discussing the difference between time management and productivity. We talked about discovering where your time goes, setting goals, and planning to achieve them.

We learned how to get and stay organized. We learned the importance of concentration and focus and explored strategies for eliminating distractions.

We discovered that procrastination has something to tell us, and we learned how to work with procrastination.

Does anyone have any questions about yesterday's modules?

Team Activity: Solving Productivity Challenges

 Facilitator: Distribute Handout 5.1: Solving Productivity Challenges.

 Show Overhead 5.1: Solving Productivity Challenges.

> **Solving Productivity Challenges**
>
> - Discover where your time goes.
> - Reduce time wasters.
> - Get organized.
> - Develop focus.
> - Make friends with procrastination.
>
> 5.1   © 2001 Patricia Haddock

Instructions to Participants: When we started the workshop yesterday, each team wrote out a list of time management challenges, which were posted on the walls around the room.

Working with your team, go over your list from yesterday and create strategies for each of these productivity challenges your team listed. If we haven't covered the challenge yet, leave it for later.

You have ten minutes for this exercise. If you finish before the time is up, you can work on other team's challenges listed on the wall.

 Facilitator: Circulate while people work on this activity.

Debriefing: Call the room to order, and ask for teams to volunteer their strategies for the next fifteen minutes.

SOLVING PRODUCTIVITY CHALLENGES

Productivity Challenge	Solutions

INTRODUCE MODULE 5: UNDERSTANDING WORK STYLES (2 MINUTES)

 Show Overhead 5.2: Understanding Work Styles.

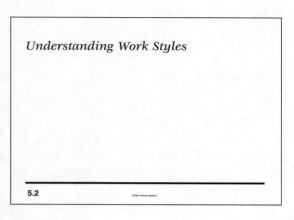

Commentary

In this module, we are going to cover work styles. When you ask people to identify the major cause of most distractions, interruptions, and irritations at work, they respond "people." Since none of us can work in solitude and most of us don't even have a door to close, it's important that we learn how people work and how we can better work with them. We also need to know how we work and how our personal work styles affect both our productivity and effectiveness and that of others.

There are no good or wrong styles, just different styles. People don't set out to drive us crazy. We feel stress and experience craziness when we don't understand why people act the way they do and when they act in ways that don't support us. Understanding work styles can give you insight into your own way of working and that of others so you can improve communication and decrease conflicts on and off the job.

OBJECTIVES FOR MODULE 5 (3 MINUTES)

 Show Overhead 5.3: Objectives for Module 5.

In this module, you will:

- Learn how to work with people who have different work styles.

- Understand how energy patterns affect productivity and how to schedule tasks accordingly.

- Understand what motivates others to take action and how to communicate with others to get things done.

ENERGY PATTERNS (15 MINUTES)

 Show Overhead 5.4: Larks and Owls.

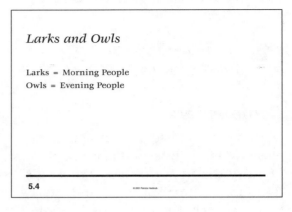

Larks and Owls

Larks = Morning People
Owls = Evening People

5.4

Commentary

Are you a lark—a morning person who jumps out of bed at 4 ᴀ.ᴍ., ready to go? By 8 ᴀ.ᴍ., you're going strong. Come noon, you're in your stride. But by 4 ᴘ.ᴍ., you're wilting. And by 9 ᴘ.ᴍ., you're in bed.

Maybe you're an owl—a night person who can't function before 10 ᴀ.ᴍ. and hits your stride at 2 ᴘ.ᴍ. By 8 ᴘ.ᴍ., you're ready for another four hours of activity. Finally, by midnight or 2 ᴀ.ᴍ., you're sleepy and ready for bed.

Are you a lark or an owl?

As you can see, these two work styles are diametrically opposed to each other. Understanding how your body's internal clock is set can help you boost productivity by showing you how to schedule your time most effectively. The more you match your activities to your energy levels, the more you can accomplish.

No matter how sophisticated we have become technologically, we are still at the mercy of our bodies. Unlike computers that can run twenty-four hours a day seven days a week, the human body is subject to rising and falling cycles during the twenty-four–hour period we call a day. The cycles are known as circadian rhythms. They make sure your body is aligned with the hours of the day so that both are in sync. Has anyone ever suffered from jet lag? Jet lag occurs when our circadian rhythms are skewed, and our body is aligning itself with a different time zone than the one we have moved into.

The most noticeable cycle is the sleep cycle. Hormones also follow cycles, as do processes such as digestion. Where we are in a cycle determines how alert we are, how energetic we feel, and how much we can accomplish during that part of the cycle. For example, experiments have shown that when people get half the amount of sleep they need, their performance suffers as if they were drunk. Light also affects cycles, both how much light we are exposed to and when we get it. For example, exposure to light energizes us, which is why many people need to sleep in darkened rooms. Those dark rooms also make it harder to wake up.

By understanding how cycles work, we can plan our days to take advantage of highs and lows. And we can assign tasks to employees to take advantage of their most productive, creative times of the day.

 Facilitator: Refer participants to Handout 1.2: Time Log.

Use a time log such as the one in Handout 1.2 for a few days to discover your energy peaks and valleys. You can use the priority column in Handout 1.2 to rank your energy level. Keep track of two types of energy: (1) how you feel mentally, your mental alertness, and (2) how you feel physically. You will be able to identify what activities you should be performing during your peak hours. Are you investing peak productivity time doing what is most important, or are you wasting it on administrative or low-priority tasks?

Use the information to schedule your time appropriately for maximum productivity. Set aside your peak hours for difficult and/or creative work that contributes most to your high-priority goals. Make an appointment with yourself to ensure that these hours are invested for maximum return. Schedule less important activities for off-peak hours.

If possible, refuse to compromise your peak hours. Don't let other people intrude on them. Don't schedule meetings, make routine calls, or allow distractions and/or interruptions.

Learn to recognize and respect other people's peak hours, especially people who report to you. Allow staff members to set their schedules to take advantage of their most productive hours.

Ask for questions.

Group Discussion

Sometimes, you just can't schedule according to your productive hours. What do you do if you are a lark and have to attend an important evening function, or if you are an owl and need to get up at 5 A.M. for a 7 A.M. presentation to key clients? Let's go over some of the characteristics of larks and owls and see how we can use this information to schedule tasks more effectively. Do any of these statements apply to you?

- *You generally awaken before or at dawn.*   Yes   No

Larks are early risers, often up before dawn. For them, sleeping in means getting up at 8 A.M. Owls, on the other hand, are at their best with a later wake-up time of 9 A.M. or even 10 A.M. because they go to bed much later than larks. What can owls do if they have to get up earlier than their biological clocks like?

 Facilitator: Lead a group discussion for a few minutes, brainstorming solutions. Ask the owls in the room to comment on the proposed solutions.

- *You enjoy eating breakfast and usually leave time for it.*   Yes   No

Larks usually enjoy breakfast and allow time for it. Owls will also do so if they can arise when their body clocks say it's time to get up. If an owl has to get up earlier than her body likes, she usually doesn't want anything to eat. Just coffee is fine. However, a meal with protein in it can help boost alertness and help wake up an owl.

What can owls do if they have to get up early? Is breakfast an option? What should they eat?

Facilitator: Lead a group discussion for a few minutes, brainstorming solutions. Ask the owls in the room to comment on the proposed solutions.

- *You feel alert and energetic before 10 A.M.*   Yes   No

Larks are usually the first ones on the job. They like early morning meetings and activities that require alertness. They should schedule presentations and make important decisions in the early morning. Owls have a hard time with activities that require alertness or energy at that time. They don't start to function at their best until late morning or early afternoon. This is the best time for activities that require them to be at their best.

What can owls do to be more effective early in the day?

Facilitator: Lead a group discussion for a few minutes, brainstorming solutions. Ask the owls in the room to comment on the proposed solutions.

- *You feel sleepy around 1 P.M.*   Yes   No

By 1 P.M., larks are starting to fade. They have been up since dawn—or earlier—and after lunch, their energy is at its lowest. They don't like activities that require concentration or alertness at that time. Owls, however, are moving into their most productive hours of the day and are ready to tackle creative, challenging activities.

What can larks do if they need to be creative or alert after lunch?

Facilitator: Lead a group discussion for a few minutes, brainstorming solutions. Ask the larks in the room to comment on the proposed solutions.

- *You don't like meetings scheduled after 3 P.M.*   Yes   No

Larks have very low energy by late afternoon. It is very hard for them to concentrate or interact in a meaningful way. Owls, on the other hand, are highly productive at that time.

What can larks do if they have a late afternoon meeting?

Facilitator: Lead a group discussion for a few minutes, brainstorming solutions. Ask the larks in the room to comment on the proposed solutions.

- *You're usually in bed by 10 P.M.—often earlier.*   Yes   No

Larks need to go to bed early because they arise so early in the morning. It is hard for them to stay awake after their regular bedtime. Owls are just the opposite. They can't fall asleep earlier in the evening. Going to bed earlier means they will just lie there, wide awake.

What can larks do if they have to stay up later than their bodies prefer?

 Facilitator: Lead a group discussion for a few minutes, brainstorming solutions. Ask the larks in the room to comment on the proposed solutions.

Commentary

Whether you are a lark or an owl, there are certain things you can do to maximize your style.

 Facilitator: Distribute Handout 5.2: Checklist for Larks and Owls.

- Schedule your day to maximize your peak energy hours.
- Set and adhere to a regular wake-up time.
- Get exposure to sunlight within fifteen minutes of awakening. Sunlight energizes your body and starts your internal clock ticking.
- If you feel your energy flagging during the day, go outside or find a window and stand or sit in sunlight for fifteen minutes.
- Schedule creative activities and activities that require intense concentration for times when your energy is high, usually the three or four hours after awakening.
- Exercise regularly.
- Take a catnap midway through the day.
- Schedule activities that require attention to detail for the hour before lunch.
- Schedule meetings for 11 A.M., when most people are alert and reasoning skills are good. Scheduling meetings just before lunch also means that you are more likely to end on time. Avoid meetings right after lunch.
- Eating protein helps raise alertness. Carbohydrates contribute to relaxation. Plan lunch and dinner based on what you need to do afterward. If you have an important meeting or presentation, order chicken or fish and avoid pasta. Avoid heavy, calorie-laden meals if you need to keep your energy up. The heavier the meal, the sleepier you will feel afterward.
- Do not skip meals. Hunger can adversely affect performance and create feelings of stress and anxiety.
- Schedule routine and/or repetitive activities for the hour right after lunch since your energy will be lowest at this time. Avoid activities that require accuracy or attention to detail.

CHECKLIST FOR LARKS AND OWLS

❑ Schedule your day to maximize your peak energy hours.

❑ Set and adhere to a regular wake-up time.

❑ Get exposure to sunlight within fifteen minutes of awakening. Sunlight energizes your body and starts your internal clock ticking.

❑ If you feel your energy flagging during the day, go outside or find a window and stand or sit in sunlight for fifteen minutes.

❑ Schedule creative activities and activities that require intense concentration for times when your energy is high, usually the three or four hours after awakening.

❑ Exercise regularly.

❑ Take a catnap midway through the day.

❑ Schedule activities that require attention to detail for the hour before lunch.

❑ Schedule meetings for 11 A.M., when most people are alert and reasoning skills are good. Scheduling them just before lunch also means that you are more likely to end on time. Avoid meetings right after lunch.

❑ Eating protein helps raise alertness. Carbohydrates contribute to relaxation. Plan lunch and dinner based on what you need to do afterward. If you have an important meeting or presentation, order chicken or fish and avoid pasta. Avoid heavy, calorie-laden meals if you need to keep your energy up. The heavier the meal, the sleepier you will feel afterward.

❑ Do not skip meals. Hunger can adversely affect performance and create feelings of stress and anxiety.

❑ Schedule routine and/or repetitive activities for the hour right after lunch since your energy will be lowest at this time. Avoid activities that require accuracy or attention to detail.

❑ Just before heading home, plan the next day.

❑ Late afternoon is best for exercising since coordination is good at this time. Exercising later in the day also contributes to restfulness and a good night's sleep.

❑ A snack of carbohydrates before bedtime can induce sleepiness.

❑ Avoid alcohol and caffeine just before bedtime.

❑ Go to bed the same time every night to keep your internal clock on time.

- Just before heading home, plan the next day.
- Late afternoon is best for exercising since coordination is good at this time. Exercising later in the day also contributes to restfulness and a good night's sleep.
- A snack of carbohydrates before bedtime can induce sleepiness.
- Avoid alcohol and caffeine just before bedtime.
- Go to bed the same time every night to keep your internal clock on time.

Ask for questions.

- -

Break: Take a five-minute stretch break.

- -

MOTIVATION STYLES (15 MINUTES)
Commentary

Understanding what motivates people is crucial to getting things done.

Has anyone spoken to a group or led a team and found yourself unable to motivate some people no matter what you did?

People respond differently to different situations. Whether you manage people or work on teams, once you know why people do what they do, you can communicate with them in a way that gets results.

Some of the information in this module comes from neurolinguistic programming (NLP), which is the study of how people achieve results. In NLP, metaprograms are internal programs, like software, that people use to process information and decide what to pay attention to. They determine what motivates us. When you understand someone's metaprograms, you can communicate with him or her more effectively.

 Show Overhead 5.5: Motivation Styles.

> **Motivation Styles**
>
> - Toward/away from
> - Internal/external
> - Self/other
>
> 5.5   © 2001 Pamela Haddock

We're going to discuss three pairs of styles:

1. Toward/away from
2. Internal/external
3. Self/other

Let's start with toward/away from.

Toward vs. Away-From Styles

This is the classic carrot versus stick approach. People with a "toward" style are goal-oriented and are motivated by the pleasure they will get when they achieve a goal or reward. They want the carrot. Toward-oriented people know what they want and are willing to take risks to get it. They are the ones who sell the most widgets in order to win the trip to Paris. Many high achievers, managers, and leaders have a toward style. Because they may be motivated solely by achieving their goals, they may be less interested in the process of achieving the goal. Toward-oriented people can also be controlling and may dominate teams.

The "away-from" style is the opposite. People with this style dislike problems and difficulties, know what they don't want, and will work to avoid it. They act to avoid the pain because they don't want the stick!

Away-from–oriented people don't respond well to goals but rather act in order to avoid the consequences of not acting. They tend to be more cautious than toward-oriented people. However, they also find it harder to maintain motivation. With this style, as soon as the pain or threat is mitigated, they lose motivation and stop acting.

Here are a couple of examples:

- A toward person goes to the dentist because he wants attractive, healthy teeth. An away-from person goes to the dentist because he doesn't want cavities.

- A toward person wants to achieve a 98 percent accuracy rate. An away-from person aims for a 2 percent error factor.

- A toward person wants to lose twenty-five pounds to look better and be healthier. An away-from person wants to lose twenty-five pounds so he won't have a heart attack or stroke.

In each example, the results are the same, but the reasons for acting—the motivation styles—are very different.

Ask for questions.

Now let's talk about internal/external.

Internal vs. External Styles

The next pair is internal/external. Internal people do a good job for the sake of doing a good job. They define their own standards, don't need external validation or feedback, and may feel stifled or annoyed when given input about their performance. They like to make decisions on their own and may resent what they perceive as interference when others try to influence them or tell them what to do.

External people, on the other hand, need feedback and validation that they are doing a good job. They tend to need more instructions, direction, and follow-up than internal people. Without external validation, they aren't sure they are doing a good job and may settle for a so-so result.

External people also have a strong desire to please and may take on more than they can handle. They have a hard time saying "no." Managers may have to monitor their workload to ensure that they can do all they have taken on.

Ask for questions.

Here are a few examples:

- An internal person will meet the production goal just to do a good job. An external person will meet the production goals if there is feedback along the way.

- An internal person will go to the dentist because it is the right thing to do. An external person will go to the dentist so that people will admire her brilliant smile.

Ask for questions.

Now let's talk about self/other.

Self vs. Other Styles

The final pair is self/other. A self-oriented person acts for her own benefit. She sells the most widgets because she wants to go to Paris. She is most interested in her own well-being.

Other-oriented people, however, act for the benefit of others. They sell the most widgets because they want to take their family to Paris. They may be altruistic and want to make things easier or better for others. Other-oriented people are often good team players and usually make excellent customer service employees, whereas self-oriented people may have problems working effectively with others and may be better at jobs that require less interaction with others.

Here are some examples:

- A self-oriented person will meet the production quota because he wants the reward that goes with meeting it. An other-oriented person will meet the production goal because he wants to share the reward with others.

- A self-oriented person will go to the doctor for a checkup because she wants to be healthy. An other-oriented person will go to the doctor for a checkup because she wants to make sure she is healthy in order to take care of her family.

Ask for questions.

Most people are more strongly one over the other in each pair, and one style dominates most activities. You may have a toward style when it comes to career and an away-from style for relationships.

What is your work style? How do you work best? Understanding your own style can help you express goals that motivate you. For example, if you have an away-from style, you always want to list the drawbacks of not achieving your goals. What do you lose? What do you not attain if you don't meet your goals?

If you have an external style, working alone with no feedback does not motivate you. You need input from others, so working on teams or with a partner may be best for you.

Understanding others' styles can help you work better with them. Keep in mind that people don't usually change. It is up to you to learn strategies to help you work more effectively with people who have styles different from your own. Once you know what pushes their buttons and gets them going, you can communicate in ways that motivate them to act. For example, if you work with a toward-oriented person, you know that you need to clearly articulate goals. If you work with a self-oriented person, you need to relate the benefits of achieving the goals to him personally.

Individual Exercise: Finding Your Motivation Style

 Facilitator: Distribute Handout 5.3: What's Your Motivation Style?

Instructions to Participants: Working alone, identify five achievements that you are proud of. They can be work-related or personal. Maybe you are proud of getting your driver's license at sixteen or graduating from college or getting a sports scholarship. Think about what motivated you to achieve these things. Did you learn how to drive because you wanted freedom or independence or because you didn't want your parents to drive you around? Did you graduate from college because you wanted to earn a degree or because your family expected you to get a degree? For each achievement, select one dominant motivation style. Then select your overall style. For example, you may discover that in three out of the five achievements, you acted with a toward, internal style and four out of five times you showed a self-orientation. Your styles are probably *toward-internal-self.* You have ten minutes for this exercise.
Ask for questions.

 Facilitator: Circulate in the room while people work on the exercise.

Debriefing: Call the room to order and ask for volunteers to describe their styles.

What are the styles of the people you work with? You can identify people's styles by paying attention to their language and behavior. Do they talk about goals or consequences? Are they self-assured, or do they seek external reinforcement? Do they talk about what they want or what they can do for others?

Sometimes, it's hard to tell. If you don't know what style a person is, it's always best to include all styles when you communicate with her. For example, clearly define a goal and include the drawbacks of not achieving it so that you appeal to both toward and away-from people. Carefully watch the person's

WHAT'S YOUR MOTIVATION STYLE?

Instructions: Working alone, identify five achievements that you are proud of. They can be work-related or personal. Maybe you are proud of getting your driver's license at sixteen or graduating from college or getting a sports scholarship. Think about what motivated you to achieve these things. Did you learn how to drive because you wanted freedom or independence or because you didn't want your parents to drive you around? Did you graduate from college because you wanted to earn a degree or because your family expected you to get a degree? Identify your dominant motivation styles for each event and your overall pattern.

Event	Toward or Away From	Internal or External	Self or Other

My dominant motivation styles are:

responses. You will know when you are getting your point across and when you aren't. You can also ask questions that elicit their style, such as "How do you know when you have done a good job?" and "What is it about [this] that interests you?" Their reply will tell you much about their style.

WORKING WITH OTHER PEOPLE (15 MINUTES)
Team Activity: Working with Other People

 Facilitator: Distribute Handout 5.4: Working with Other People.

 Show Overhead 5.6: Work Styles.

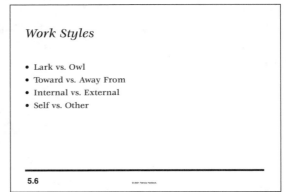

Work Styles

• Lark vs. Owl
• Toward vs. Away From
• Internal vs. External
• Self vs. Other

5.6   © 2001 Patricia Haddock

Instructions to Participants: This handout describes the work styles of four different employees and whether they are larks or owls. Working with your team, decide how you will communicate with these employees to achieve the goals outlined in the exercise. Consider things such as the best time of day to meet with the people, the language you will use, and the arguments you will put forth to convince them to act in the way you want them to act.

For example, in Case Study 1, Sally is a lark, with a toward-internal-self style. Your goal is to motivate Sally to form and lead a team to plan the office United Way campaign. How would you communicate to Sally in a way that motivates her? You have fifteen minutes for this exercise. Work on as many case studies as you have time for.

Ask for questions.

 Facilitator: Circulate among teams while they work on this exercise.

Debriefing: Call the room to order and ask for teams to share their strategies. Make sure you get input on each of the four case studies.

Break: We're now going to take a fifteen-minute break. Please return at [time].

WORKING WITH OTHER PEOPLE

Instructions: This handout describes the work styles of four different employees. Working with your team, decide how you will communicate with these employees to achieve the goals outlined in the exercise. Consider things such as the best time of day to meet with the people, the language you will use, and the arguments you will put forth to convince them to act in the way you want them to act.

Case Study 1: Sally is a lark, with a toward-internal-self style. How would you approach her to form and lead a team to plan the office United Way campaign?

_____

_____

Case Study 2: Henry is an owl with an away-from–external–other style. He has recently been promoted to your supervisor. How would you approach him to ask for a raise?

_____

_____

Case Study 3: Carlos is a lark with a toward-external-other style. How would you convince him to take a CPA class that would improve his chances for promotion?

_____

_____

Case Study 4: Janella is an owl with an away-from–internal–other style. How would you convince her to accept a lateral transfer to a new job with more responsibility but no additional pay?

_____

_____

Understanding Work Styles—Notes

Review Day One	
Objectives for Module 5	
Energy Patterns	Lark Owl
Motivation Styles	Toward/Away From Internal/External Self/Other
Working with Other People	

MASTERING MEETINGS
(1.5 HOURS)

OBJECTIVES FOR MODULE 6

- Plan and lead more productive meetings.
- Reduce time spent in meetings.
- Accomplish more in less time.
- Communicate more effectively in groups.
- Create teamwork, consensus, and support.
- Improve the quality of meetings.

MATERIALS NEEDED

- Handout 6.1: The Top 10
- Handout 6.2: Meeting Planner Worksheet
- Handout 6.3: Sample Agenda
- Handout 6.4a: Sample Small Meeting Room Setup
- Handout 6.4b: Sample Small to Moderate Meeting Room Setup
- Handout 6.4c: Sample Large Meeting Room Setup
- Handout 6.5: Rate Yourself as a Meeting Leader
- Handout 6.6: Reading Body Language
- Handout 6.7: Solutions to Reading Body Language

- Handout 6.8: How Would You Manage This Meeting Challenge?
- Handout 6.9: Meeting Evaluation
- Handout 6.10: Checklist for Attending a Meeting
- Overhead 6.1: Mastering Meetings
- Overhead 6.2: Objectives for Module 6
- Overhead 6.3: Types of Meetings
- Overhead 6.4: Creating Visual Aids and Handouts
- Overhead 6.5: Meeting Leader Responsibilities
- Overhead 6.6: Presenting with Power
- Overhead 6.7: Stimulating Participation
- Overhead 6.8: Managing Conflict and Confrontation
- Overhead 6.9: Handling Difficult People
- Overhead 6.10: Managing Conflict and Confrontation
- Overhead 6.11: Managing Conflict and Confrontation (continued)
- Overhead 6.12: Attending a Meeting

AGENDA

Review Module 5	10 minutes
Planning the Meeting	35 minutes

- Objectives for Module 6
- Why Meetings Don't Work
- Reasons for and Types of Meetings
- Getting Ready to Meet
- Creating Effective Visual Aids and Handouts

Leading the Meeting	35 minutes

- Rating Yourself as a Meeting Leader
- Running the Meeting
- Presenting with Power
- Stimulating Participation
- Reaching Decisions
- Handling Difficult People
- Managing Conflict and Confrontation

After the Meeting	5 minutes
Attending a Meeting	5 minutes

REVIEW MODULE 5 (10 MINUTES)

 Facilitator: Welcome people back from the break and bring the room to order.

Team Activity: The Top 10 Strategies for Working with Others

 Facilitator: Distribute Handout 6.1: The Top 10.

Instructions to Participants: Working with your team, identify the Top 10 strategies you learned in Module 5: Understanding Work Styles for working effectively with others. Then, each person on your team should choose three strategies you intend to implement as soon as you return to work. You have ten minutes.

 Show Overhead 6.1: Mastering Meetings.

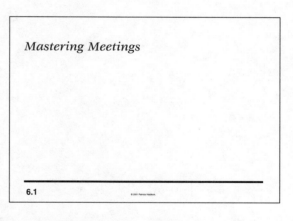

PLANNING THE MEETING (35 MINUTES)

Commentary

According to the Wharton Center for Applied Research, the typical manager spends seventeen hours a week in meetings and another six hours preparing for them, but only 56 percent of these meetings are productive. This means that managers waste more than fifteen hours a week in meaningless meetings. That's more than sixty hours a month. What would you do with an extra sixty hours a month?

THE TOP 10

Instructions: Working with your team, identify the Top 10 strategies you learned for working effectively with others. Then, each member of the team should choose three strategies to implement when you return to work.

1.

2.

3.

4.

5.

6.

7.

8.

9.

10.

Your three strategies:

1.

2.

3.

Objectives for Module 6

Show Overhead 6.2: Objectives for Module 6.

Learning how to plan and lead more productive meetings can give you several extra hours each week.
   This module will teach you how to:

- Communicate more effectively in groups.

- Reduce time spent in meetings.

- Create teamwork, consensus, and support.

- Accomplish more in less time.

- Improve the quality of meetings.

Objectives for Module 6

- Communicate more effectively in groups.
- Reduce time in meetings.
- Create teamwork, consensus, and support.
- Accomplish more in less time.
- Improve the quality of meetings.

6.2

Why Meetings Don't Work
Group Discussion

Meetings often don't work for several reasons. The most common are the lack of clearly defined objectives, lack of an agenda, and/or failure to follow the agenda. What are some other reasons meetings don't work?
   Lead a group discussion about why meetings don't work. Some topics to cover are poor planning, poor leadership, lack of an agenda, failure to follow an agenda, and poor facilities and/or equipment.

Reasons for and Types of Meetings
Commentary

Meetings are not an end unto themselves. They are an effective means of sharing information or reaching a decision.

Show Overhead 6.3: Types of Meetings.

Information meetings are used to impart information. Sales presentations are considered information meetings. In general, attendance at information meetings is limited to people who need to know the

Types of Meetings

- Information meetings
- Decision-making meetings
- Regular meetings

6.3

information. These meetings are primarily presentation-style meetings, with ample opportunities for questions and answers. Emphasis is on delivery of content.

Decision-making meetings are used for goal setting, problem solving, and production of a deliverable. They work best when the number of attendees is limited since their success relies on interaction and discussion among participants. Strong leadership skills are needed to keep discussions on target, yet allow for creativity and spontaneity.

Regular meetings, such as monthly staff meetings, may actually be a drain on productivity. In order for regular meetings to be meaningful, they need to satisfy one of the two reasons for meeting: (1) impart information, or (2) reach a decision. If they don't meet these requirements, find an alternative that is more efficient than meetings.

Group Discussion

Lead a group discussion about alternatives to meetings and when each would be appropriate. What might some alternatives be? A group email can be used to communicate information where group input is not necessary. A group voicemail or email can be used for announcements.

Getting Ready to Meet

 Facilitator: Distribute Handout 6.2: Meeting Planner Worksheet.

Commentary

This worksheet can help you plan every meeting you lead. We are going to go through some of the items on the worksheet now so you can understand how to use it.

Effective, productive meetings start with planning. Begin by identifying meeting objectives. Meeting objectives should be measurable and specific so that you can evaluate the meeting's effectiveness and determine whether the meeting is necessary. Can the objectives be met without a meeting? If so, how? If you must hold a meeting, define specific measures you will use to evaluate the effectiveness of this meeting.

You also need to decide where and when the meeting will occur. Generally, meetings should not go longer than ninety minutes. If a meeting needs to go longer, build in frequent breaks and activities.

Determine meeting date and time.

- Meet before lunch if a decision needs to be made. Hunger is a good incentive to cut to the chase and get things done.

- Start meetings at an odd time—on the quarter hour, or 8:15 A.M. or 8:20 A.M. rather than 8:00 A.M. This can improve punctuality.

MEETING PLANNER WORKSHEET

1. What are your objectives for this meeting? Can the objectives be met without a meeting?

2. State specific measures you will use to evaluate the effectiveness of this meeting.

3. Set the date, time, and location for the meeting.

4. Identify participants who need to attend by using the following criteria:

   - What contribution will this person make?
   - Is it essential that this person attend in person?
   - Is this the best person to attend the meeting?
   - Can this person send a designee in his or her place?
   - Does this person have to be present for the entire meeting? Can he or she drop in and then leave?

5. Create and publish a meeting agenda that includes all of the following information:

   - Objectives for the meeting.
   - Date, time, and location, and directions to the meeting site, if necessary.
   - Discussion items, discussion leaders, and time frames for each discussion.
   - Breaks, if appropriate.

6. Invite participants.

7. Determine and see to the following:

   - Meeting room setup, i.e., conference room style, classroom style, lecture style, etc.
   - Electronic equipment, i.e., overhead projector, LCD screen, microphones, VCR, etc.
   - Materials, i.e., name tags, handout copies, notebooks, pencils, etc.
   - Refreshments, if appropriate.

8. Leading the meeting:

   - Arrive early and ensure that the room is set up properly, electronic equipment is there and works, and materials are ready for distribution.
   - Greet participants as they arrive.
   - Begin on time.
   - State the objectives for the meeting.
   - Follow the agenda.

- Introduce each agenda item and the participant leading the discussion.
- Encourage participation.
- Allow time for discussions, and keep them on track.
- Provide summaries and feedback.
- Assign tasks and responsibilities for follow-up.

9. End the meeting on time.

10. Evaluate the effectiveness of the meeting based on measures defined.

11. Create and distribute meeting record with follow-up actions and tasks defined and assigned.

- Avoid meeting late in the afternoon. This is not a good idea since most people hit an energy low between 2:00 P.M. and 4:00 P.M.

- Avoid meeting on the day before a holiday or weekend, since people will be more focused on their upcoming time off than on business.

Determine meeting location. Location is very important to the success of a meeting. Some of the things to consider are:

- Size and seating capacity of the room
- Lighting and ventilation
- Distractions
- Furnishings
- Equipment

Invite the fewest number of people possible. Identify who should attend the meeting by using the following criteria:

- What contribution will this person make?
- Is it essential that this person attend?
- Is this the best person to attend the meeting?
- Can this person send a designee in his place?
- Does this person have to be present for the entire meeting, or can she drop in for her agenda item and then leave?

Ask for questions.

 Facilitator: Distribute Handout 6.3: Sample Agenda.

Commentary

Create and publish a meeting agenda in advance of the meeting. Depending on the objectives, you may need to develop the agenda with key participants. The agenda should be organized so that you achieve your stated objectives, and it should include all of the following information:

- Date, time, and location
- Directions to the meeting site, if necessary
- Objectives for the meeting
- Items to be discussed, and who will lead each discussion
- Time frames for each discussion
- Breaks, if appropriate

An agenda ensures that the meeting stays on target and meets its objectives. It focuses participants on key issues and allows them to prepare in

SAMPLE AGENDA

DATE: November 3, 2000

TIME: 9:15 A.M.–10:30 A.M.

LOCATION: Apollo Building, Conference Room 19-C
(19th floor, opposite the mail room)

OBJECTIVES:

- Help managers understand the new health care plan so they can explain it to their employees.
- Describe enrollment procedures.
- Provide materials for managers to give to employees.

Time	Topic	Person Responsible
9:15 A.M.	Start meeting	Ms. Connors
9:15 A.M.–9:30 A.M.	Introduce new plan	Ms. Barrows
9:30 A.M.–9:50 A.M.	Show videotape	Ms. Connors
9:50 A.M.–10:00 A.M.	Explain enrollment procedures	Ms. Connors
10:00 A.M.–10:15 A.M.	Questions	Ms. Barrows
10:30 A.M.	Conclude meeting	Ms. Barrows

Please confirm your attendance by October 30. If you cannot attend, please send someone to represent your unit.

advance. Redistribute the agenda at the start of the meeting and review it with participants at that time.

Don't expect people to read and digest volumes of information at the meeting itself. Mail lengthy documents ahead of time with the agenda. If you are distributing confidential information, ensure that only the addressee receives it and understands the need to maintain confidentiality.

Ask for questions.

Invite participants by phone and follow up with meeting details, a copy of the agenda by mail or email, and a list of participants. Whenever possible, give people enough time to prepare for the meeting, especially if they are making a presentation.

Ask for questions.

Make physical arrangements for the meeting:

- Make arrangements for any necessary electronic equipment, e.g., overhead projector, LCD screen, microphones, VCR.

- Arrange for materials, e.g., name tags, handout copies, notebooks, pencils.

- Order refreshments, if appropriate.

Ask for questions.

Facilitator: Distribute Handout 6.4a: Sample Small Meeting Room Setup, Handout 6.4b: Sample Small to Moderate Meeting Room Setup, and Handout 6.4c: Sample Large Meeting Room Setup.

Commentary

The right room setup and equipment can contribute to meeting success. If you require participants to break into smaller groups, make sure the tables and chairs allow for easy movement. Avoid classroom setup if you want participation. A good general room setup for most meetings is the "U" shape, with participants arranged around a head table that holds equipment. Your handouts show the most effective meeting room setup based on numbers of participants.

Ask for questions.

Creating Effective Visual Aids and Handouts
Commentary

According to 3M, researchers have discovered that presentations are 43 percent more effective when visual aids are used. Many presenters use presentation software such as PowerPoint® to create overheads or slides with talking points. These software products allow you to reformat the overheads to use as handouts.

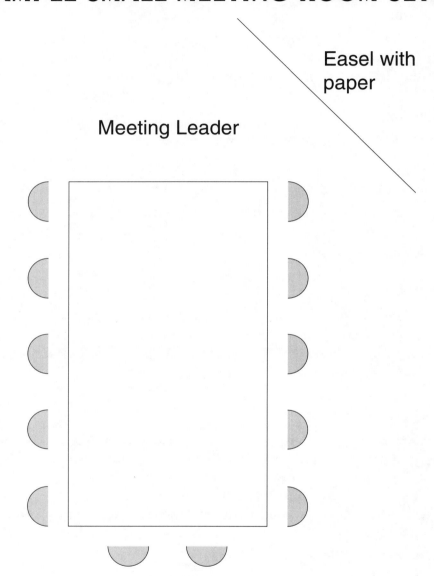

SAMPLE SMALL MEETING ROOM SETUP

Easel with paper

Meeting Leader

Refreshments

SAMPLE SMALL TO MODERATE MEETING ROOM SETUP

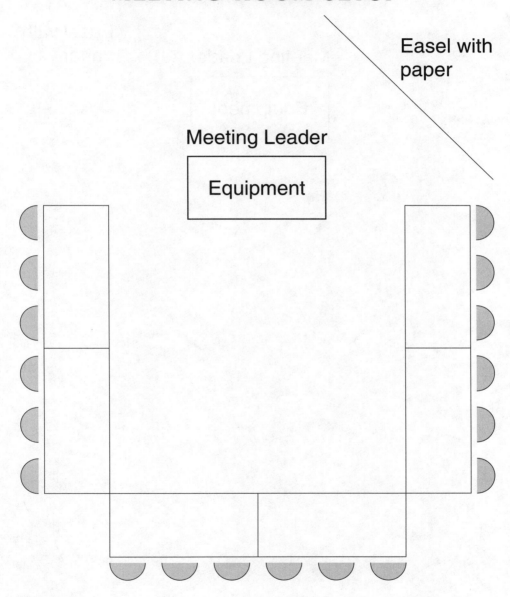

Easel with paper

Meeting Leader

Equipment

Refreshments

SAMPLE LARGE MEETING ROOM SETUP

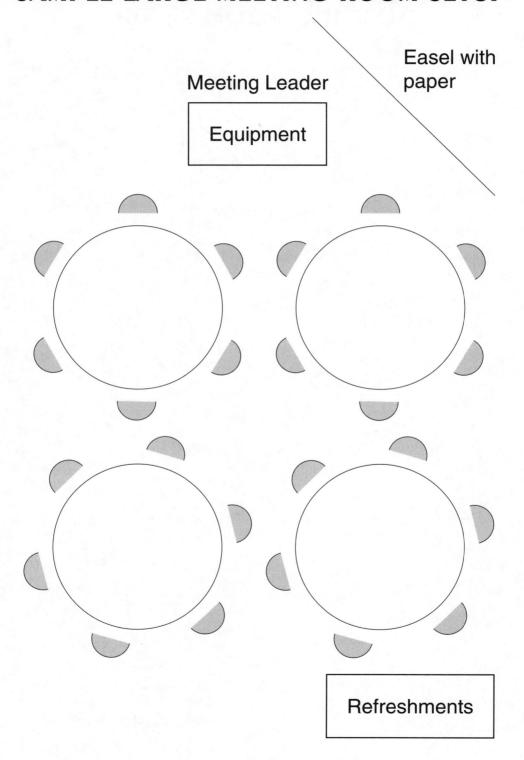

Remember: Technology is not foolproof. What can go wrong will. Make sure you have a backup plan in case the projector or the computer dies.

 Show Overhead 6.4: Creating Visual Aids and Handouts.

> *Creating Visual Aids and Handouts*
>
> - Simple and easy to read
> - Large typefaces and fewer than seven lines
> - Use of talking points
> - Use of clip art and color
> - Respect for copyright protection
>
> 6.4

Here are some things to remember about visual aids and handouts:

- Keep visual aids and handouts simple and easy to read.
- Use large typefaces—at least twenty points—on visual aids.
- Don't cram too much on each slide or overhead. Don't use more than seven lines of type per slide.
- Use talking points on the slides or overheads, not entire sentences.
- Use clip art, where appropriate, to enliven materials.
- Do not violate copyright by copying protected cartoons or artwork.

Ask for questions.

Team Activity: Preparing Overheads

 Facilitator: Break participants into their teams, and pass out markers, white paper, and masking tape.

Instructions to Participants: Look at the "Leading the meeting" section of Handout 6.2: Meeting Planner Worksheet. Using the paper and markers, prepare a set of overheads that could be used for this part of the module. After you have completed your set of overheads, use the masking tape and tape your overheads on the wall nearest your team. You have ten minutes for this activity.

Ask for questions.

Debriefing: Use the overheads developed by the class to illustrate points in this section of the program. Ask the team that created each overhead to discuss their overheads with the class.

LEADING THE MEETING (35 MINUTES)
Rating Yourself as a Meeting Leader

 Facilitator: Distribute Handout 6.5: Rating Yourself as a Meeting Leader.

RATING YOURSELF AS A MEETING LEADER

When you lead a meeting . . .	Yes	Sometimes	No
The meeting begins on time.			
Everyone has a chance to express his or her opinion.			
I use an agenda to keep the meeting on track.			
The meeting ends on time.			
A meeting record is kept and published.			
Clear responsibility for follow-up actions is determined.			
A/V equipment works properly.			
Handouts contribute to the meeting objectives.			
I encourage fewer vocal participants to get involved.			
I resolve conflicts before they escalate.			
I require feedback from participants.			
I stimulate discussion.			
Overheads can be read from the back of the room.			
The agenda goes out ahead of the meeting.			
I keep assertive participants from controlling the meeting.			

Total _____

Score: Give yourself 5 points for every "Yes," 3 points for every "Sometimes," and 0 points for every "No." The higher your score, the stronger your meeting leader skills. Pay attention to every item you marked "Sometimes" or "No." These are areas where you can sharpen your meeting skills and become more productive.

Individual Exercise: Rating Yourself as a Meeting Leader

Instructions to Participants: Before we go into the meeting process itself, take a few minutes to rate yourself as a meeting leader. This assessment will help you understand where your strengths are and where you need improvement in making meetings work.

Running the Meeting

 Show Overhead 6.5: Meeting Leader Responsibilities.

> **Meeting Leader Responsibilities**
>
> * Monitor content.
> * Provide direction.
> * Encourage interaction.
> * Create atmosphere of cooperation.
> * Move the meeting forward.
>
> 6.5

Commentary

The meeting leader's primary task is to meet the stated objectives for the meeting. You do this by:

* Ensuring that the content of the meeting stays on target
* Providing direction for discussions
* Encouraging interaction
* Creating an atmosphere of openness and cooperation
* Moving the meeting process forward

The meeting actually starts before participants arrive. As the meeting leader, you need to set aside time before the meeting to prepare. You must:

* Decide what you want to say.
* Develop and copy handouts and overheads.
* Rehearse your presentation, especially if you are nervous speaking to a group.

You need skills for presenting information, answering questions, leading discussions, and handling conflict.

As the meeting leader, you should arrive at least fifteen minutes before the start of the meeting. Make sure the room is set up as you requested, you have the materials you need, and refreshments have arrived. Test electronic equipment to make sure it works and projection equipment is in focus. Make sure A/V material can be seen from every part of the room. Set out materials such as name tags, notebooks, etc. The earlier you arrive for the meeting, the easier it will be to set up and have any problems corrected before people begin arriving.

Start the meeting on time, even if people are absent. Delaying the start of the meeting encourages people to come late next time. You may have to juggle the agenda if people who are scheduled early in the meeting arrive late. You may want to designate someone as timekeeper or ask for a volunteer.

Always restate the objectives, ask for agreement from participants, and review the agenda. Have participants introduce themselves and briefly state their role.

Generally, you want to follow the agenda, but you need to adapt the agenda if a discussion is proving fruitful and contributes to the objectives. Some people need more time to process information and require more discussion than others. While you want to honor the agenda, you also want to make sure that everyone has an opportunity to contribute and be heard. If time looks like it will run out before the objectives are met, ask for the group's input before altering the agenda.

Ask for questions.

Presenting with Power

 Show Overhead 6.6: Presenting with Power.

Commentary

Leading a meeting is more than talking at people. You need to master both verbal and nonverbal communication skills. Speak clearly and concisely in a moderate tone and with a moderate pace. Vary your tone and pitch to create variety.

Presenting with Power

• Verbal skills
• Nonverbal skills

6.6

Don't ramble. Make sure that your comments are relevant and keep things moving. Never read from your notes. Know your topic well enough to speak only by referring to notes.

What you don't say may be more important than what you do say. One "silent" way of communicating that you are the meeting leader is to take the chair at the head of the table or to stand at the opening of a U-shaped room setup.

Maintain an erect posture, and stand when speaking. If possible, move around the room to hold people's attention.

Maintain regular eye contact with everyone, allowing your gaze to move around the room and include everyone. Don't bounce your gaze around. Let it rest for five to seven seconds before moving on.

Team Activity: Reading Body Language

 Facilitator: Distribute Handout 6.6: Reading Body Language.

READING BODY LANGUAGE

Instructions: Match the behavior described in the first column with the body language in the second column.

Behavior	Body Language
Steepled hands, hands behind back, hands in pockets	Openness
Open hands, unbuttoned jacket	Nervousness
Short breaths, clenched hands, wringing hands	Defensiveness
Pinching flesh, chewing gum, biting fingernails	Confidence
Arms crossed, rubbing nose and eyes, drawing away	Insecurity
Open hands, sitting on edge of chair, leaning forward	Frustration
Clearing throat, fidgeting, jiggling keys or money	Cooperation
Sitting/moving back, arms folded, head down	Engaged
Arms behind back, smiling, open stance	Listening
Head tilted, eye contact, nodding	Defiant
Closes papers, pen down, hands on table	Desire to speak
Hands on hips, frowning	Evaluating
Leaning forward, foot tapping, finger pointing	Desire to leave
Finger tapping, staring	Aggressive
Leaning forward, open body, open arms	Ready to agree
Sucks glasses/pen, looks right and left, crossed legs	Attentive
Feet toward door, looking around, buttoning jacket	Rejection

Instructions to Participants: Read Handout 6.6: Reading Body Language. Then, working with your team, match the behavior in the first column with the body language in the second column. You have ten minutes for this exercise.

 Facilitator: Distribute Handout 6.7: Solutions to Reading Body Language.

Debriefing: Call the room to order and discuss the correct answers.
Ask for questions.

Break: Take a five-minute stretch break.

Stimulating Participation

 Facilitator: Call the room to order.

 Show Overhead 6.7: Stimulating Participation.

Commentary

There are many different ways you can stimulate participation. We'll discuss three of them: brainstorming, brain drain, and drawing people out.

> *Stimulating Participation*
>
> • Brainstorming
> • Brain drain
> • Drawing people out
>
> _____
>
> **6.7**

1. *Brainstorming.* One way of drawing people out is brainstorming, which is often used to generate diverse ideas or options. This is a process where the meeting leader clearly states the problem or situation; everyone voices ideas without criticism, judgment, or evaluation; and someone records all the ideas on a flipchart or whiteboard. After the brainstorming session, the group discusses the ideas generated and begins evaluating them. The emphasis in brainstorming is quantity of ideas.

2. *Brain Drain.* Another technique is the nominal group conference, or brain drain. With this process, participants take turns writing their responses to a question posed to the whole group. The meeting leader calls on each person who gives one of his ideas, which is recorded on a flipchart or whiteboard. After everyone has had a chance to speak, additional input is solicited from the entire group. The process continues until the group runs out of ideas. Then, each participant ranks her Top 10 ideas. Rankings from the whole group are then combined to create a Top 10 list for the group. You can use this technique with a larger

SOLUTIONS TO READING BODY LANGUAGE

Behavior	Body Language
A. Steepled hands, hands behind back, hands in pockets	Confidence
B. Open hands, unbuttoned jacket	Openness
C. Short breaths, clenched hands, wringing hands	Frustration
D. Pinching flesh, chewing gum, biting fingernails	Insecurity
E. Arms crossed, rubbing nose and eyes, drawing away	Defensiveness
F. Open hands, sitting on edge of chair, leaning forward	Cooperation
G. Clearing throat, fidgeting, jiggling keys or money	Nervousness
H. Sitting/moving back, arms folded, head down	Rejection
I. Arms behind back, smiling, open stance	Attentive
J. Head tilted, eye contact, nodding	Listening
K. Closes papers, pen down, hands on table	Ready to agree
L. Hands on hips, frowning	Defiant
M. Leaning forward, foot tapping, finger pointing	Aggressive
N. Finger tapping, staring	Desire to speak
O. Leaning forward, open body, open arms	Engaged
P. Sucks glasses/pen, looks right and left, crossed legs	Evaluating
Q. Feet toward door, looking around, buttoning jacket	Desire to leave

group by breaking into smaller groups and having each smaller group work on a problem, then report their findings to the whole group.

3. *Drawing People Out.* You can also ask people about their opinion and reaction to something in order to draw them out. Use open-ended questions that require more than a yes or no answer. Questions that begin with "What" or "How" usually solicit responses. When you ask a question, pause for about twenty seconds to give people time to think of a response and gather their thoughts.

You can call on people to summarize what was said, clarify points, and give examples. A good way to encourage participation and obtain feedback at the same time is to ask each participant how he feels the meeting is going.

Group Discussion

We have used several different techniques to stimulate participation during this workshop. What are some of them?

Lead a group discussion to identify techniques used in the workshop. The class has used:

- Asking questions
- Asking people to share experiences
- Having people work in small teams
- Brainstorming ideas

Reaching Decisions

 Show Overhead 6.8: Reaching Decisions.

Reaching Decisions

- Define problem/situation.
- Recap information.
- Discuss options.
- Ask for a decision.
- Communicate decision.

6.8

Commentary

Often, you need the group to make a decision. Most decisions involve an element of risk or uncertainty, which could be mitigated by ensuring that the group has discussed all viable options, and people feel comfortable that they have the information they need to make the decision. Make sure you allow time in the agenda for the decision-making process to run its course. Some people may require more time to digest information and make decisions than others. Some need supporting data before making up their minds. If this happens, you may need to adjourn and reconvene later when they have had time to absorb this additional information.

We will learn more about effective decision making in Module 7: Decision Making and Setting Priorities. For now, the following steps will help you develop your decision-making skills:

- Define the situation or problem, and ask if everyone agrees with your statement. If not, clarify the statement until everyone agrees.
- Recap information necessary for making a decision, and ask the group if they have enough information. If not, have them define what they need.
- Discuss the options and their ramifications, including short-term versus long-term consequences, the pros and cons, and other issues, such as resources needed to implement the decision, costs, etc.
- Ask for a decision using one of the following methods:
  - *Voting:* Ask for a show of hands. The majority wins.
  - *Polling:* Go around the room, ask each person's opinion, and address any reservations to create buy-in.
  - *Nominal group technique:* After discussing alternatives, members rank each. Scores for each alternative are added, and the lowest scoring alternatives are eliminated. The process is repeated with the highest scoring alternatives until a single choice remains.
  - *Consensus:* This is an interactive process. The goal is not unanimity but rather acceptance of the chosen alternative. There are no losers—rather, you are looking for an alternative acceptable for everyone. Use logic and business reasons to support each position, not feelings and emotions. Expect differences of opinion, and encourage people to express themselves. This is the only way a consensus can be reached.
- Decide how the decision will be communicated to affected parties.

Ask for questions.

Handling Difficult People

 Show Overhead 6.9: Handling Difficult People.

Commentary

Difficult people can be negative, irritating, and impossible to deal with. They can create havoc at a meeting and cause contention and confrontation. You need to really listen to what is said in order to handle a difficult person effectively. Let's look at some of the more common types of difficult people you will encounter and discuss some strategies for handling them.

Handling Difficult People

- Long-winded people
- Bulldozers
- Know-it-alls
- Sneaks
- Naysayers

6.9

Long-winded people. These people monopolize meeting time and can alienate other people. What are some strategies you can use with these people?

Question: Ask the group to name strategies that can be used with long-winded people. List suggestions on a flipchart or whiteboard.

Answer: Start with a nonverbal "stop" sign, such as holding up one hand, palm toward the speaker. Smile. Use language such as "That's a good point, Roger. Let's hear what others think." If this approach doesn't work, be firmer. Remind the speaker of the meeting objectives and where you are in the agenda. State that you have to move on; then do so.

Bulldozers. Bulldozers are often aggressive and rude. What are some strategies you can use with these people?

Question: Ask the group to name strategies that can be used with bulldozers. List suggestions on a flipchart or whiteboard.

Answer: Address them by name and refuse to argue or get in a shouting match. Give them room to vent; then ask them to calm down. You may have to ask them to leave or take a break to let them calm down.

Know-it-alls. These people are often subject experts who can contribute value to a meeting. However, they tend to take over if not properly managed. What are some strategies you can use with these people?

Question: Ask the group to name strategies that can be used with know-it-alls. Write suggestions on a flipchart or whiteboard.

Answer: Respect their knowledge and ask questions of them, but don't allow them to "take over." Give them an opportunity to share their knowledge.

Sneaks. These people often use sarcasm and make negative comments under their breath, but just loudly enough to be disruptive. What are some strategies you can use with these people?

Question: Ask the group to name strategies that can be used with sneaks. Write suggestions on a flipchart or whiteboard.

Answer: Your best defense is to expose them with direct questions. They often retreat if directly queried.

Naysayers. These people look for what is wrong with an idea or solution. What are some strategies you can use with these people?

Question: Ask the group to name strategies that can be used with naysayers. Write suggestions on a flipchart or whiteboard.

Answer: A certain amount of criticism is good, but these people typically refuse to find anything positive. Keep them focused on facts, and steer them away from their negative opinions.

Managing Conflict and Confrontation

 Show Overhead 6.10: Managing Conflict and Confrontation.

> **Managing Conflict and Confrontation**
>
> - Don't take sides.
> - Stop nonconstructive disputes.
> - Stay calm and objective.
> - Use "I" sentences.
>
> 6.10

Commentary

Even if everyone has agreed on a goal, disagreements can occur. Conflict can also occur because of personality differences, power struggles, and personal agendas.

Conflict can be constructive if it leads to good solutions and new ideas. Allow conflict to run its course as long as it is productive. If it ceases to be productive, or if conflict is nonconstructive at the start, stop it immediately. Constructive conflict leads to discussion and creative problem solving. Destructive conflict is divisive and negative.

Here are some suggestions for handling nonconstructive conflicts:

- Avoid taking sides.
- Stop disputes when they start. Use language such as "I don't think we can resolve this now, so I am asking that we move on."
- React calmly and objectively.
- Use "I" statements to avoid accusations. Make sure others use "I" statements too. For example, "You're always late" is a "You" statement that puts the other person on the defensive. An "I" statement, such as "I would like you to be on time for meetings," is better. Another example is, "Your solution won't work." A better statement is, "I would like to try a different solution, since I'm not convinced this is the best one."

 Show Overhead 6.11: Managing Conflict and Confrontation (continued).

> **Managing Conflict and Confrontation (continued)**
>
> - Ask questions.
> - State outcomes.
> - Resolve the conflict or table the discussion.
> - Take a break.
>
> 6.11

- Ask questions that require the other person to talk about the situation.
- State what each person wants as an outcome.
- Agree on a resolution or table this discussion if the conflict cannot be resolved.
- Take a break if tempers are hot.

Ask for questions.

Team Activity: Managing a Meeting Challenge

 Facilitator: Distribute Handout 6.8: How Would You Manage This Meeting Challenge?

Instructions to Participants: For the next fifteen minutes, work with your team and develop a strategy for handling the meeting challenge summarized in the handout.

Debriefing: Call the room to order. Ask for one to three teams to report on the strategy they developed.

AFTER THE MEETING (5 MINUTES)

 Facilitator: Distribute Handout 6.9: Meeting Evaluation.

Commentary

End the meeting on time. Make sure you recap decisions that were made and review assignments. Record action items, responsible parties, and a date and method for follow-up. Summarize action items before leaving the meeting for clarity.

Remind participants that you will be publishing a meeting record. If appropriate, schedule the date and time of a follow-up meeting. You may also want to ask people to complete a meeting evaluation form, such as the one in Handout 6.9.

Prepare a memo that summarizes decisions, lists action items, and reminds participants of any items requiring follow-up.

ATTENDING A MEETING (5 MINUTES)

 Show Overhead 6.12: Attending a Meeting.

 Facilitator: Distribute Handout 6.10: Checklist for Attending a Meeting.

Commentary

What should you do when you are asked to attend a meeting?

> *Attending a Meeting*
>
> - Do you have to attend?
> - Enter the meeting on your calendar.
> - Ask for an agenda.
> - Gather information.
> - Prepare.
> - Offer to take minutes.
> - Keep the meeting on track.
>
> 6.12

HOW WOULD YOU MANAGE THIS MEETING CHALLENGE?

Instructions: You are leading a meeting to introduce a new flexible time schedule for staff. Marge, a manager who is very critical of the new schedule, is constantly interrupting the speakers with negative comments and questions designed to challenge the speakers' expertise. You are starting to fall behind the agenda, and people are becoming restless and irritable. Some people are starting to agree with Marge's criticisms of the new schedule. One of your objectives for meeting is to gain the support of managers so the new schedule is positively positioned to employees. How will you handle this situation?

MEETING EVALUATION

Meeting:

Date: _____   Length:

Answer the following questions to evaluate the effectiveness of your meeting:

1. Were meeting objectives achieved?   Yes   No

2. Did the meeting begin on time?   Yes   No

3. Did the meeting end on time?   Yes   No

4. Did participants have a chance to express themselves? Yes   No

5. Did participants seem satisfied with the meeting?   Yes   No

6. Were disputes resolved fairly?   Yes   No

7. Were participants encouraged to participate?   Yes   No

8. How can the meeting be improved?

CHECKLIST FOR ATTENDING A MEETING

What should you do when you are asked to attend a meeting?

☐ Find out if you have to attend in person. Can you send someone else? Do you have to attend the entire meeting, or can you attend the relevant part and then leave?

☐ Note the meeting on your calendar, and allow travel time. Make sure you include the location of the meeting and the name and phone number of your primary contact.

☐ Ask for an agenda to be sent to you before the meeting.

☐ Start a file for what you will need to take with you.

☐ If you are making a presentation, make sure you schedule time to prepare.

☐ Offer to take minutes. This gives you an excuse to keep things on track.

☐ If the meeting leader doesn't keep the meeting on track, gently move things along using statements such as "Can we discuss this offline?" "Before we move on, can we summarize where we are?" "I think we are off track. Can we return to the point we were pursuing?"

- Find out if you have to attend in person. Can you send someone else? Do you have to attend the entire meeting, or can you just attend relevant parts and then go?
- Note the meeting on your calendar, and allow travel time. Make sure you include the location of the meeting and the name and phone number of your primary contact.
- Ask for an agenda to be sent to you before the meeting.
- Start a file for what you will need to take with you.
- If you are making a presentation, make sure you schedule time to prepare.
- Offer to take minutes. This gives you an excuse to keep things on track.
- If the meeting leader doesn't keep the meeting on track, gently move things along using phrases such as "Can we discuss this offline?" "Before we move on, can we summarize where we are?" "I think we are off track. Can we return to the point we were pursuing?"

Ask for questions.

Break: We're going to take a one-hour lunch break now. Please return at [time.] We will start the next module promptly.

Mastering Meetings—Notes

Review Module 5	
Objectives for Module 6	
Why Meetings Don't Work	Reasons why meetings don't work:

Reasons for and Types of Meetings	Information Decision making
Getting Ready to Meet Creating Effective Visual Aids and Handouts	Determine objectives Create measures Identify participants Publish agenda Decide logistics
Leading the Meeting	Meeting leader responsibilities:
Presenting with Power	Verbal skills Nonverbal skills

Stimulating Participation	Brainstorm
	Brain drain
	Drawing people out
Reaching Decisions	Define problem/situation
	Recap information
	Discuss options
	Ask for a decision
	Voting
	Polling
	Nominal group technique
	Consensus
	Communicate decision
Handling Difficult People	

Managing Conflict and Confrontation	
After the Meeting	
Attending a Meeting	

Decision Making and Setting Priorities (1 hour)

OBJECTIVES FOR MODULE 7

- Understand the decision-making process.
- Learn strategies for making decisions more quickly and confidently.
- Take calculated risks.
- Identify and evaluate alternatives and relative risks.

MATERIALS NEEDED

- Handout 7.1: Seven Steps to More Effective Decision Making
- Handout 7.2: Checklist for Evaluating Options
- Handout 7.3: What Do You Do?
- Overhead 7.1: Decision Making and Setting Priorities
- Overhead 7.2: Objectives for Module 7
- Overhead 7.3: Seven Steps to More Effective Decision Making

AGENDA

Review Module 6	10 minutes
Decision Making and Setting Priorities	5 minutes
Objectives for Module 7	5 minutes
Seven Steps to More Effective Decision Making	40 minutes

REVIEW MODULE 6 (10 MINUTES)

 Facilitator: Welcome participants back from lunch.

Group Discussion

In Module 6: Mastering Meetings, we discussed four ways of making decisions at meetings. Who can tell us what those four decision-making processes were?

 Facilitator: Ask for volunteers and write their answers on a flipchart or whiteboard.

1. *Voting:* Ask for a show of hands. The majority wins.
2. *Polling:* Go around the room, ask each person's opinion, and address any reservations to create buy-in.
3. *Nominal group technique:* After discussing alternatives, members rank each. Scores for each alternative are added, and the lowest scoring alternatives are eliminated. The process is repeated with the highest scoring alternatives until a single choice remains.
4. *Consensus:* This is an interactive process. The goal is not unanimity but rather acceptance of the chosen alternative. There are no losers; rather, you are looking for an alternative acceptable for everyone. Use logic and business reasons to support each position, not feelings and emotions. Expect differences of opinion, and encourage people to express themselves. This is the only way a consensus can be reached.

Team Activity: Decision-Making Processes

Instructions to Participants: Module 7 deals with the decision-making process. Before we start the module, working with your team, create one overhead that could be used for each of the four decision-making processes for meetings. Create your overhead using the criteria we discussed in Module 6. You have five minutes for this exercise.

 Facilitator: Pass out plain paper and marking pens.

Debriefing: Call the room to order. Ask for volunteers to show and read the overheads they developed.

INTRODUCE MODULE 7: DECISION MAKING AND SETTING PRIORITIES (5 MINUTES)

 Show Overhead 7.1: Decision Making and Setting Priorities.

Decision Making and Setting Priorities
7.1

Group Discussion

Your ability to make decisions is a key factor in your ability to be productive and effective. It is an important time management skill. Why is that?

Lead a brief discussion on why decision making is an important time management skill. Typical answers include:

- Ability to make decisions means projects can move forward and deadlocks are avoided.

- Decision making also forces people on what needs to be done and reduces the likelihood of false starts or false trails.

OBJECTIVES FOR MODULE 7 (5 MINUTES)

 Show Overhead 7.2: Objectives for Module 7.

Objectives for Module 7
• Understand the decision-making process. • Learn strategies for making decisions more quickly and confidently. • Take calculated risks. • Identify and evaluate alternatives and relative risks.
7.2

Commentary

In this module, you are going to learn the elements of the decision-making process and discover how you can make better decisions. You will:

- Understand the decision-making process.
- Learn strategies for making decisions more quickly and confidently.
- Take calculated risks.
- Identify and evaluate alternatives and relative risks.

SEVEN STEPS TO MORE EFFECTIVE DECISION MAKING (40 MINUTES)

Commentary

Most of the decisions you make are no-brainers—what to have for lunch, whether to take the car or public transportation, what to wear to work.

What are some of the easy work-related decisions you have to make? Ask for answers from volunteers.

Some decisions, however, are tough and complex and may affect other people both on and off the job. They require you to weigh options and evaluate the consequences of each.

What are some of the tough work-related decisions you have to make? Ask for answers from volunteers.

 Show Overhead 7.3: Seven Steps to Effective Decision Making.

 Facilitator: Distribute Handout 7.1: Seven Steps to More Effective Decision Making.

> *Seven Steps to Effective Decision Making*
>
> 1. Defining the goal
> 2. Gathering facts and information
> 3. Developing potential options
> 4. Evaluating options
> 5. Selecting an option
> 6. Implementing your decision
> 7. Evaluating your decision
>
> _____
>
> **7.3**   © 2001 Patricia Haddock

There are seven steps to effective decision making:

1. Defining the goal
2. Gathering facts and information
3. Developing potential options
4. Evaluating options
5. Selecting an option
6. Implementing your decision
7. Evaluating your decision

Let's discuss each step.

Step 1: Defining the Goal

Commentary

A decision is a means to an end, not the end itself. Sometimes, we forget this. Your objective is not to make a decision but to achieve a goal. The process starts by identifying the goal.

Identifying what you want to accomplish determines the kind of decision you need to make. Let's say you want to hire someone to mow your lawn because you want to spend more time with your family and less time on lawn

SEVEN STEPS TO MORE EFFECTIVE DECISION MAKING

1. Defining the goal
2. Gathering facts and information
3. Developing potential options
4. Evaluating options
5. Selecting an option
6. Implementing your decision
7. Evaluating your decision

maintenance. What's the goal? To hire someone to mow your lawn, or to spend more time with your family?

If the goal is to get someone to mow your lawn, your options and ultimate decision will be different than if your goal is to spend more time with your family. For example, if your goal is to hire someone to mow your lawn, you need to evaluate different people who want to do this job, decide what skills they need to have, and decide how much to pay them. On the other hand, if your goal is to spend more time with your family, you may not need someone to mow the lawn at all. You could plant slow-growing grass so the lawn doesn't have to be mowed so often. You could replace the lawn with gravel, redwood chips, or low-maintenance plants. You could make lawn care a family event and do it with your kids and spouse.

Defining the right goal is very important in the decision-making process. We talked about SMART goals in Module 1: Time Management and Productivity and in Module 2: Getting Organized. What is a SMART goal? Ask for answers.

The goal you define should be a SMART goal. How can SMART goals keep you on track and on time? Ask for answers.

Step 2: Gathering Facts and Information
Commentary

The next step is to gather facts and information to help you develop options. You may need to talk to others—especially people who will be affected by the decision—read source documents, and go on the Internet to conduct research.

Sometimes, we spend a lot of time on this step because we are avoiding making the decision. It is important that you limit the amount of time you spend gathering information. Allow enough time to get the information you need, but don't allow so much time that it becomes an exercise in procrastination.

Ask for questions.

Step 3: Developing Potential Options
Commentary

The third step is to develop potential options. The quality of the decision you make will be determined by the quality of the options you have to choose from.

Ask yourself: What are your alternatives? Let your imagination run free here. The object is to give yourself as many alternatives as possible, so brainstorm until you run out of ideas.

Again, get input from other people who are affected by the decision. The more you involve them in the process, the more they will feel ownership for the result.

We talked about brainstorming in Module 6: Mastering Meetings. What are some factors that contribute to a good brainstorming session? Ask for volunteers to talk about brainstorming.

Ask for questions.

Step 4: Evaluating Options

 Facilitator: Distribute Handout 7.2: Checklist for Evaluating Options.

Commentary

Each option represents a different course of action and a different decision. You need to ask and answer a series of questions about each option. In order to adequately answer these questions, you may need input from other people. Here are the questions you need to ask and answer:

- What are the consequences of this option? Look for both long-term and short-term outcomes.

- How well does this option meet the goals you have identified? You may want to revisit your stated goal and decide whether it is still the right goal or if you need to modify it.

- What effect does this option have on other people? How does the option affect other areas of your life or work?

- Is this option ethical? Does it reflect your values and those of your company? Would you feel comfortable if this option were to be made public knowledge?

- What are the trade-offs of this option? You need to understand clearly what you gain and lose with each option since it is unlikely that one option will be perfect.

- What are the risks associated with this option? How much risk can you handle? What could you potentially lose? Make sure you understand the worst-case scenario and are willing to accept it as a possibility.

- How much will the option cost in time, money, staff, resources, and so on? Relative costs are an important factor to consider.

- How does this option help you achieve better results? Does it help you achieve your goals faster?

- What is the likelihood of success for this option? How much uncertainty can you handle?

- Has the option been tried before? If so, what were the results? How is this situation similar? Different?

- How does this option affect future options? Does it expand or narrow future possibilities and potentialities?

CHECKLIST FOR EVALUATING OPTIONS

Each option represents a different course of action and a different decision. You need to ask and answer a series of questions about each option. In order to adequately answer these questions, you may need input from other people.

❑ What are the consequences of this option? Look for both long-term and short-term outcomes.

❑ How well does this option meet the goals you have identified? You may want to revisit your stated goal and decide whether it is still the right goal or if you need to modify it.

❑ What effect does this option have on other people? How does the option affect other areas of your life or work?

❑ Is this option ethical? Does it reflect your values and those of your company? Would you feel comfortable if this option were to be made public knowledge?

❑ What are the trade-offs of this option? You need to understand clearly what you gain and lose with each option since it is unlikely that one option will be perfect.

❑ What are the risks associated with this option? How much risk can you handle? What could you potentially lose? Make sure you understand the worst-case scenario and are willing to accept it as a possibility.

❑ How much will the option cost in time, money, staff, resources, and so on? Relative costs are an important factor to consider.

❑ How does this option help you achieve better results? Does it help you achieve your goals faster?

❑ What is the likelihood of success for this option? How much uncertainty can you handle?

❑ Has the option been tried before? If so, what were the results? How is this situation similar? Different?

❑ How does this option affect future options? Does it expand or narrow future possibilities and potentialities?

❑ Other:

Group Discussion

What other questions could you ask? Lead a brief discussion of other questions.

Ask for questions.

Step 5: Selecting an Option
Commentary

The next step is to reduce the potential options you've arrived at to the top three. Look at each of your top three options and review your answers to the previous questions. Are there any other factors you need to consider? Have you overlooked anything? Create a list of pros and cons for your top three options.

What does your intuition tell you about each option? Don't discount the feelings you get about each option. Your subconscious mind can make connections that your conscious mind cannot. Never ignore the feeling in your gut about a decision. Take time to find out where that feeling is coming from and if it raises legitimate issues you need to address before making your decision.

Ask other people for their opinion. Do they feel the same way you do? If not, why and how are they responding differently? Listen carefully to what they say.

Still can't make up your mind? Ask an objective person you respect to evaluate the options and give you her opinion. She may be able to see issues and factors you can't.

Now you can make your decision.

Ask for questions.

Step 6: Implementing Your Decision
Commentary

Implementation requires several steps:

1. Decide what action steps are needed, and assign responsibility for each of them.
2. Communicate your decision to everyone affected by it.
3. Communicate your reasons for choosing this option.
4. Find out if any people object to the decision, and handle their objections early. The sooner you get agreement from everyone involved, the easier it will be to implement the decision.

Ask for questions.

Step 7: Evaluating Your Decision
Commentary

Once you have implemented your decision, you must ask yourself: Did you make the right decision? You need to monitor the results of your decision and its implementation. What happens if the decision is wrong? Mistakes happen. The key is to acknowledge it and make a new decision. The process starts over since the decision to change your decision is a new one.

Ask for questions.

Team Activity: Making a Decision

 Facilitator: Distribute Handout 7.3: What Do You Do?

Instructions to Participants: Working with your team, take the case study on the handout through the seven steps for decision making:

1. Define the goal.
2. You won't be able to gather facts and information, so just identify where and how you would get the information you need to make your decision. Assume that you have done your research.
3. Brainstorm potential options.
4. You won't have time to evaluate all your options, so just come up with a pros and cons list for two or three options.
5. Select an option.
6. Identify the action steps that need to be taken to implement your decision and who needs to be notified.
7. You won't be able to evaluate your decision, so just come up with a list of criteria you would use to evaluate your decision.

You have twenty minutes for this exercise.

 Facilitator: Circulate the room while participants work on this exercise.

Debriefing: Call the room to order. Ask for one or two teams to review how they made their decision, summarizing their results for each step of the decision-making process.

Break: Take a fifteen-minute break.

WHAT DO YOU DO?

Instructions: Working with your team, take the case study on the handout through the seven steps for decision making:

1. Define the goal.
2. You won't be able to gather facts and information, so just identify where and how you will get the information you need to make your decision. Assume that you have done your research.
3. Brainstorm potential options.
4. Create a list of pros and cons for two or three options.
5. Select an option.
6. Identify the action steps that need to be taken to implement your decision and who needs to be notified.
7. Create the criteria you will use to evaluate your decision.

Case Study:

Selena has been offered a promotion to a position in London. She will get a small salary increase and special compensation for an overseas assignment. The new position will take her career from administration to sales. She isn't sure she wants to make the shift since sales is a new area for her. She also isn't sure she wants to live overseas. What steps can Selena take to make a decision?

_____

_____

Decision Making and Setting Priorities—Notes

Review Module 6	Voting Polling Nominal group technique Consensus
Objectives for Module 7	
Seven Steps to More Effective Decision Making	

Creating Balance and Setting Boundaries (2 Hours)

OBJECTIVES FOR MODULE 8
- Evaluate how satisfied you are with different areas of your life.
- Identify stressors that are creating an imbalance.
- Create strategies for bringing your life more into balance.
- Create a benchmark for measuring progress.
- Establish boundaries.

MATERIALS NEEDED
- Handout 8.1: Decision Making
- Handout 8.2: Life Balance Assessment
- Handout 8.3: Checklist for Setting Boundaries
- Overhead 8.1: Creating Balance and Setting Boundaries
- Overhead 8.2: Objectives for Module 8
- Overhead 8.3: Where Are You Out of Balance?
- Overhead 8.4: Setting Priorities
- Overhead 8.5: Priorities after "This-or-That" Process

- Overhead 8.6: Setting SMART Goals
- Overhead 8.7: Setting Boundaries

AGENDA

Review Module 7	20 minutes
Creating Balance and Setting Boundaries	3 minutes
Objectives for Module 8	2 minutes
Where Are You Out of Balance?	45 minutes
Picking Your Priorities	20 minutes
Setting SMART Goals	20 minutes
Setting Boundaries	10 minutes

Facilitator: Welcome participants back from the break and call the room to order.

REVIEW MODULE 7 (20 MINUTES)

 Facilitator: Distribute Handout 8.1: Decision Making.

Team Activity: Making a Decision

Instructions to Participants: Working with your team, choose one of the cases on the handout and decide how you will resolve the stalemate. You have fifteen minutes for this exercise.

Ask for questions.

Debriefing: Call the room to order, and ask for volunteers to share their solution to the case. Make sure you cover all three cases.

CREATING BALANCE AND SETTING BOUNDARIES (3 MINUTES)

 Show Overhead 8.1: Creating Balance and Setting Boundaries.

> Creating Balance and Setting Boundaries
>
> 8.1

Commentary

Where are you simply surviving, instead of thriving? Where could your life be more fulfilling? Does any part of your life seem overwhelming? A major issue facing people today is how to balance their personal and professional lives. According to a survey of U.S. workers, their number one job priority is balancing job and personal responsibilities. We find ourselves torn between job responsibilities and personal responsibilities. Often, the job wins, and the more our job wins, the more unbalanced our lives become.

When our lives are out of balance, we feel stressed. We spend more time reacting to events rather than taking charge of them. We fall into unproductive habits that undermine our confidence and self-esteem. We lose sight of what is important, or we find ourselves unable to do what is most important because we're overwhelmed with other things that "need" to get done.

On the other hand, people whose lives are balanced focus on possibilities and opportunities rather than problems and pitfalls. They live lives of passion

DECISION MAKING

Instructions: Working with your team, choose one of the following cases and decide how you will resolve the stalemate:

1. Hal is leading a team to implement a marketing campaign for a new software product. The success of the product hinges on the most effective campaign. ABC Marketing and Exeter Marketing have both responded to RFPs and are the final contenders. ABC has proposed an elaborate campaign that includes animation and high Web visibility. Exeter is taking a more moderate, traditional approach. Hal's team has been reviewing and discussing the proposals for three hours and needs to make a decision but is reluctant to commit. What steps can Hal take to help the team make a decision?

2. Mark and his partner, David, have been asked to design a Web site for a local nonprofit. Mark is eager to jump into the project since it will give the partners the chance to meet and work with several important businesspeople who could give them business. David is less eager because they currently have three major accounts to design Web sites for and are understaffed. Mark and David have been arguing for days. What steps can they take to come to a decision?

3. Steven, Pascal, Mary, Lassanda, and Hal work on a team to develop new customer service standards for their claims department. Steven and Pascal want to hold focus groups with phone contact people to get their input on the team's first draft of the new standards. Mary, Lassanda, and Hal think that no one should review the standards until management has had input. There are pluses and minuses for each approach. What steps can the team take to choose an approach?

and purpose rather than fear, frustration, and stress. They set boundaries to ensure that they spend their time doing what is most important.

Group Discussion

What does a balanced life mean to you? Ask two to three people to share their ideas.

OBJECTIVES FOR MODULE 8 (2 MINUTES)

 Show Overhead 8.2: Objectives for Module 8.

Commentary

This module will help you:

- Evaluate how satisfied you are with nine different areas of your life.

- Identify stressors that are creating an imbalance.

- Create strategies for bringing your life more into balance.

- Create a benchmark for measuring progress.

- Establish boundaries.

Objectives for Module 8

- Evaluate satisfaction with different areas of your life.
- Identify stressors.
- Create strategies for more balance.
- Create a benchmark for progress.
- Establish boundaries.

8.2   © 2001 Patricia Haddock

WHERE ARE YOU OUT OF BALANCE? (45 MINUTES)

 Show Overhead 8.3: Where Are You Out of Balance?

Commentary

As we have seen, balance means different things to different people, and the definition can change as our lives change. What we mean by balance and how we evaluate what is important to us is very personal. For

---

Where Are You Out of Balance?

- Career/Work
- Relationships/Romance
- Money Matters
- Health and Wellness
- Family/Friends
- Physical Environment
- Recreation/Rejuvenation
- Spiritual
- Personal Growth

8.3   © 2001 Patricia Haddock

---

this reason, most of the exercises in this module are private ones. You can share with your team only if you feel comfortable doing so.

In order to create balance in more areas of your life, you first need to identify how satisfied you are with what you have today in each of the following areas:

- Career/Work
- Relationships/Romance
- Money Matters
- Health and Wellness
- Family/Friends
- Physical Environment
- Recreation/Rejuvenation
- Spiritual
- Personal Growth

You need to review each area and create a benchmark for how balanced your life is now. This is the only way you can measure change. In the following exercises, you will summarize what is going on right now in each area. Pretend that you are having a candid conversation with a stranger you will never see again. Be totally honest and describe the way things are in each area of your life right now.

Individual Exercise: Is Your Life Balanced?

 Facilitator: Distribute Handout 8.2: Life Balance Assessment.

Instructions to Participants: On a scale of 1 to 10, with 1 being totally unsatisfied and 10 being totally satisfied, evaluate how satisfied you are with each of these areas of your life. Then, write a brief description of what this area is like right now. Keep in mind that you are not assessing the areas in relation to each other. You are assessing them in relation to what you would consider ideal for you in that particular area.

The term "10" implies perfection, the top, the best by *your* standards. As you assess each area of your life, use your personal definition of "10"—not what society, your parents, or your friends would select. Pay close attention to your own heart and mind. Determine what success is for you—not for anyone else. Keep in mind that life ebbs and flows. It is unlikely that anyone will have a 10 in each area all the time. Be gentle with yourself. Wherever you are right now is fine for right now.

Here are some examples:

- *Career/Work:* Betty rated Career/Work a 4. In her description, she writes that she has been working at night with her spouse in a restaurant he recently opened. Her job is suffering because she is tired every day. She

LIFE BALANCE ASSESSMENT

Instructions: On a scale of 1 to 10, with 1 being totally unsatisfied and 10 being totally satisfied, rank how satisfied you are with the following areas of your life. In the box, write a brief description of this area as it is now.

For example:

Career/Work Rating: 4 Assessment: I have been working at night with my spouse in a restaurant he recently opened. My job is suffering because I am tired every day. I enjoy my job and have the opportunity for advancement. I also want to help my husband succeed. I feel torn and unsure of what to do.	1	2	3	4 X	5	6	7	8	9	10

Write your assessment and rating here.

Career/Work Rating: Assessment:	1	2	3	4	5	6	7	8	9	10

Relationships/Romance Rating: Assessment:	1	2	3	4	5	6	7	8	9	10
Money Matters Rating: Assessment:	1	2	3	4	5	6	7	8	9	10
Health and Wellness Rating: Assessment:	1	2	3	4	5	6	7	8	9	10
Family/Friends Rating: Assessment:	1	2	3	4	5	6	7	8	9	10

Physical Environment Rating: Assessment:	1	2	3	4	5	6	7	8	9	10
Recreation/Rejuvenation Rating: Assessment:	1	2	3	4	5	6	7	8	9	10
Spiritual Rating: Assessment:	1	2	3	4	5	6	7	8	9	10
Personal Growth Rating: Assessment:	1	2	3	4	5	6	7	8	9	10

List here the three priority areas you want to work on with the highest priority listed as number one.

1. _____

2. _____

3. _____

How would each area have to change to improve its rating by two points? Here is an example: One of Marvin's three priority areas was Money Matters. Marvin gave his current Money Matters a score of 3 and wrote that he owed more than $5,000 on his credit cards and had only $200 in savings. In order to move his score from 3 to 5, Marvin decides he would have to pay off 30 percent of his credit card debt and double his savings.

Decide how your three priorities need to change to increase your rating two points:

1. _____

2. _____

3. _____

What is your number one priority? Write it here and create three SMART goals to help you achieve it.

For example, here are Marvin's SMART goals:

1. Stop using credit cards immediately and start paying cash.
2. Create and stick to a budget within thirty days from today.
3. Limit lunch and dinner out to once a month starting now.

Write your SMART goals here:

1. _____

2. _____

3. _____

enjoys her job and has the opportunity for advancement. She also wants to help her husband succeed. She feels torn and unsure of what to do.

- *Family/Friends:* Rene rated Family/Friends a 5. She and her son recently moved, and both are struggling to make new friends. She's busy learning a new job and doesn't keep in touch with her family as much as she would like.

- *Recreation/Rejuvenation:* Mike gave this area an 8. He has just returned from a week in the country where he recharged and rested after a particularly difficult time at work. He usually takes good care of himself, getting enough exercise and rest, but feels that he needs more time away to unwind and think.

It's your turn. I will read a short paragraph about each area of your life. Then you should take five minutes to rate the area and describe what is going on in that area of your life. Keep in mind: Where you are now is less important than where you want to be.

Ask for questions.

 Facilitator: Introduce each section, read the text that goes with it, and give participants five minutes to evaluate each area and describe what is going on.

- *Career/Work:* When you rank this and describe what it looks like today, consider passion for work; work lifestyle; people, places, and things you interact with; the environment you work in; your income and other benefits; your job security; and whether or not your work drains you or invigorates you.

 Facilitator: Allow five minutes; then call for participants' attention.

- *Relationships/Romance:* Consider your level of fulfillment with your significant relationship. If you are not in a significant relationship, consider your level of satisfaction with that. Do you spend enough time with your loved one, is the relationship supportive and loving, and does it invigorate you? Is there playfulness and intimacy and respect to the level you would like? Are there any sexual or reproductive issues that need to be addressed?

 Facilitator: Allow five minutes; then call for participants' attention.

- *Money Matters:* Consider your income, your expenses, your debt and debt elimination program, your credit history, your retirement plan, your insurance, how much you have in savings, how you manage your money, and your relationships with the professionals who serve you—your accountant, banker, bookkeeper or tax preparer, insurance agent.

Facilitator: Allow five minutes; then call for participants' attention.

- *Health and Wellness:* Consider your posture, weight, level of vitality, absence of aches and pains, strength, bone density, muscle mass, skin health, teeth, feet, eating, and excretory and sleep habits.

Facilitator: Allow five minutes; then call for participants' attention.

- *Family/Friends:* Consider your relationships. Are they healthy and supportive? Are they honest and communicative? Do you feel the closeness you desire? Do you spend enough time with your friends and family? Do you have enough of these kinds of relationships in your life?

Facilitator: Allow five minutes; then call for participants' attention.

- *Physical Environment:* Consider your home, car, office, and personal appearance related to your hair and wardrobe. Do you love where you live? Does the inside of your home resemble more a sanctuary or a slum? Is your car up-to-date on all maintenance? Do you feel safe in it? Is your office at home or at work in order, allowing you to easily find what you need? Do your clothes fit? Do you feel well dressed when you walk out the door? Do you like your haircut? Are your shoes shined with well-kept heels?

Facilitator: Allow five minutes; then call for participants' attention.

- *Recreation/Rejuvenation:* Do you take enough time off to play, to vacation, to do nothing? Do you have a variety of activities you enjoy outside of work? Do you have some kind of fun every day?

Facilitator: Allow five minutes; then call for participants' attention.

- *Spiritual:* Do you love yourself? Do you feel the kind of connection you would like with a higher power or with a spiritual community? Do you feel emotionally balanced, or do you feel depressed and in a panic? Is your soul full?

Facilitator: Allow five minutes; then call for participants' attention.

- *Personal Growth:* Consider your level of satisfaction with your skills, love, communication, risk taking, etc., and your level of satisfaction with how you are growing as a human being—whom you are becoming, your personal evolution.

 Facilitator: Allow five minutes; then call for participants' attention.

PICKING YOUR PRIORITIES (20 MINUTES)
Commentary

Now, rank each area of your life and decide which are your top three priorities. For example, if you were recently promoted, Career/Work may be most important. If you just inherited some money, Money Matters might be another priority right now. If your daughter just had a baby, Family/Friends might be your third priority.

 Show Overhead 8.4: Setting Priorities.

> **Setting Priorities**
>
> A. Career/Work
> B. Money Matters
> C. Family/Friends
> D. Physical Environment
> E. Health and Wellness
>
> _____
>
> 8.4   © 2001 Pamela Hardick

A good way to determine priorities is to use a "This-or-That" process. List the areas you are considering as candidates for your top three priority list, and assign each a letter of the alphabet. Then, compare A with B and decide which is more important. Using this example, let's say Marvin takes his list and compares A with B and chooses B as more important. He then compares B with C and again chooses B. He continues this process through the entire list and chooses B each time. When he finishes the list, he makes B his number one priority. He does the process again, this time starting by comparing A with C. Let's say C is more important. Marvin then compares C with D and chooses D as the more important priority. He then compares D with E and chooses D. D now becomes his number two priority.

Show Overhead 8.5: Priorities after "This-or-That" Process.

> **Priorities after "This-or-That" Process**
>
> 1. Money Matters
> 2. Physical Environment
> 3. Family/Friends
> 4. Health and Wellness
> 5. Career/Work
>
> ───────────────────────────
>
> **8.5**   © 2001 Patricia Haddock

When Marvin finishes with the "This-or-That" process, his new list looks like this.

Now it's your turn. Using the "This-or-That" process, go back to Handout 8.2 and decide which areas you would rate as your three priorities. You have five minutes for this.

Ask for questions.

Facilitator: Call the room to order.

Refer back to your assessment of these three areas. Are you satisfied with your ratings in each of them? If so, congratulations. Make sure that you continue to pay attention to these areas to stay in balance and direct your attention to what's most important. Are there any other areas you want to improve that are not in your top three? If so, choose your top priority among those areas.

How would each of the areas you have chosen to work with need to change in order to improve their rating by two points? Here's an example: Marvin gave his current Money Matters a score of 3 and wrote that he owed more than $5,000 on his credit cards and had only $200 in savings. It would be difficult for Marvin to move his score from 3 to 10. It is much easier for him to move it two points, from 3 to 5. How would this area have to change in order for Marvin to increase his rating by two points?

Group Discussion

Lead a group discussion on this question and encourage a variety of responses.

Individual Exercise: Improving Your Ratings

Instructions to Participants: Now it's your turn to describe how the three areas you chose would have to change if they were to go up two points in your evaluation. Notice your thoughts and what you say as you work through this process. If you find yourself saying, "I should," you're usually hearing the voice of someone else. "I should lose weight" is probably not *you* talking. It could be your mother, your spouse, or Madison Avenue. Your own voice probably sounds more like "I want to lose weight" or "I am going to lose weight." Replace every "I should" with "I want." You have fifteen minutes for this exercise.

Ask for questions.

Debriefing: Call the room to order. Ask for volunteers who are willing to share what they wrote.

SETTING SMART GOALS (20 MINUTES)

 Show Overhead 8.6: Setting SMART Goals.

Commentary

Just knowing what your priorities are isn't enough. You need to set SMART goals for each of them to ensure that the changes you need to make occur.

> *Setting SMART Goals*
>
> - <u>S</u>pecific: Spell out each goal in detail.
> - <u>M</u>easurable: You need to evaluate success.
> - <u>A</u>daptable: Goals need to respond to what's happening in your life.
> - <u>R</u>ealistic: Blue sky, but be real!
> - <u>T</u>imely: Put a deadline on each goal.
>
> 8.6   © 2001 Patricia Haddock.

 Facilitator: Ask for a volunteer to remind the group of what SMART goals are. Refer to Module 1: Time Management and Productivity, if necessary.

Group Discussion

In our earlier example, let's say Marvin decides to reduce his credit card debt. What are some goals he could set?

Lead a group discussion of what SMART goals Marvin could set to pay down his credit card debt. Some points to cover are:

- Stop charging by a certain date.
- Research debt consolidation.
- Look at lower interest rate cards.

Individual Exercise: Setting Your SMART Goals

Now go back to Handout 8.2. Take your number one priority and set three SMART goals to help you achieve that priority. You have fifteen minutes for this exercise.

Ask for questions.

 Facilitator: Call the room to order.

Debriefing: You need to set SMART goals for each of your three priority areas. We don't have time to do this now, but I encourage you to take the time to do so after the workshop.

Facilitator: Refer participants to Handout 1.5: Setting SMART Goals.

At the beginning of the workshop, you set career goals. Please go back to that handout and look at those goals. Are there any conflicts between them and the goals you just set in this module? If so, you need to reevaluate and decide what's most important to you. This is a most important step to ensure that you achieve your goals with a minimum of stress and conflict.

Stress often occurs when you ignore what is most important to you and spend time on goals that are less important. If you have a conflict among your goals, schedule time on your calendar to consider your options and decide the right priority for your goals.

SETTING BOUNDARIES (10 MINUTES)
Commentary

Now that you have determined your priorities, you need to make sure you act in ways that are consistent with them. For example, if Career/Work is your number one priority, you will make different decisions about working long hours and on weekends than someone whose number one priority is Family/Friends. Imbalance comes from making many little choices that take you farther from your most important goals. Over time, the accumulation of these choices affects the satisfaction you feel with every aspect of your life.

As we have learned, we experience stress when we make decisions and act in ways that are in conflict with our priorities. It is important that we set and maintain boundaries to ensure that our priorities are respected and our goals attained.

 Facilitator: Distribute Handout 8.3: Checklist for Setting Boundaries.

 Show Overhead 8.7: Setting Boundaries.

> **Setting Boundaries**
>
> - Communicate.
> - Learn to say "no."
> - Be treated fairly and with honesty.
> - Require respect.
> - Refer to your top three priorities and goals.
> - Be flexible and respond to the moment.
>
> 8.7

Here are some things you need to do to set boundaries:

- Communicate openly with others and let them know what the boundaries are. Don't set traps for people. Let them know what your priorities are so they understand what you will and won't do. This is especially important for telecommuters. Often, family and friends think that because you are working at home, you are available to run errands and visit with them. You need to define clearly what work is and what socializing is when you work at home.

CHECKLIST FOR SETTING BOUNDARIES

❏ Communicate.

❏ Learn to say "no."

❏ Insist that you be treated fairly and with honesty.

❏ Require others to respect their commitments to you.

❏ Keep your top three priorities and their respective goals where you can see them and refer to them when you are unsure about committing your time to an activity.

❏ Be flexible and let yourself respond to the moment. Spontaneity can be healthy and creative.

❏ Other:

- Learn to say "no." This can be hard to do, but by not saying "no," we commit to activities that we really don't want to do. You can soften your response by giving people your reasons for saying "no" and, where possible, offer an alternative. Don't allow yourself to feel guilty for standing by your priorities, and don't allow yourself to be bullied into doing something. Remember: When you say "no" to someone, you are saying "yes" to something else. Make sure that something else is important and has value for you.

- Insist that you be treated fairly and with honesty.

- Require others to respect their commitments to you.

- Keep your top priorities and their respective goals where you can see them and refer to them when you are unsure about committing your time to an activity.

- Be flexible and let yourself respond to the moment. Spontaneity can be healthy and creative. Let yourself set aside plans and priorities if it feels right to do so. If you do this often, review your priorities and goals to determine if they are still right for you or if you need to make some changes.

Break: We're going to take a fifteen-minute break now. Please return at [time].

Creating Balance and Setting Boundaries—Notes

Review Module 7 Creating Balance and Setting Boundaries	
Objectives for Module 8	

Where Are You Out of Balance?	Career/Work
	Relationships/Romance
	Money Matters
	Health and Wellness
	Family/Friends
	Physical Environment
	Recreation/Rejuvenation
	Spiritual
	Personal Growth
Picking Your Priorities	
Setting SMART Goals	<u>S</u> <u>M</u> <u>A</u> <u>R</u> <u>T</u>
Setting Boundaries	

Managing Time on the Road and Course Assessment (1 Hour)

OBJECTIVES FOR MODULE 9

- Plan travel more efficiently to reduce mishaps and wasted time.
- Reduce stress associated with traveling.
- Make the most of time on the road.

MATERIALS NEEDED

- Handout 9.1: Checklist for Becoming a Time-Savvy Traveler
- Handout 9.2: Travel Master List
- Handout 9.3: Certificate of Achievement
- Handout 9.4: Course Assessment
- Overhead 9.1: Managing Time on the Road
- Overhead 9.2: Objectives for Module 9
- Overhead 9.3: Time Management Strategies
- Overhead 9.4: Course Assessment

AGENDA

Review Module 8	10 minutes
Managing Time on the Road	3 minutes
Objectives for Module 9	2 minutes
Becoming a Time-Savvy Traveler	10 minutes
Creating a Master List	10 minutes
Time Management Strategies	15 minutes
Course Assessment	10 minutes

Facilitator: Welcome participants back from the break and call the room to order.

REVIEW MODULE 8 (10 MINUTES)

 Facilitator: Refer participants to Handout 8.3: Checklist for Setting Boundaries.

Team Activity: Setting Boundaries

Instructions to Participants: Before the break, we covered some strategies for setting boundaries. Work with your team to add to this list. What can you do to set boundaries so that you can better concentrate on your priorities? You have ten minutes for this exercise.

Ask for questions.

Debriefing: Call the room to order. Ask for some teams to volunteer what they added to their list.

INTRODUCE MODULE 9: MANAGING TIME ON THE ROAD AND COURSE ASSESSMENT (3 MINUTES)

 Show Overhead 9.1: Managing Time on the Road.

Group Discussion

Have you ever been on a business trip and discovered that you left an important document at the office? Maybe it was the diskette with your handouts or a key table that didn't get copied. Maybe you left your itinerary on your dresser at home. Everyone has a horror story of a trip gone bad because of poor planning.

> **Managing Time on the Road**
>
> 9.1   © 2001 Patricia Haddock

Ask for three or four participants to share stories.

OBJECTIVES FOR MODULE 9 (2 MINUTES)

 Show Overhead 9.2: Objectives for Module 9.

> *Objectives for Module 9*
>
> - Reduce mishaps and wasted time.
> - Reduce stress.
> - Make the most of time on the road.
>
> 9.2   © 2001 Patricia Haddock

Commentary

Travel is, by its nature, stressful. Without careful planning, travel can be torture. In this module, you will learn how to:

- Plan travel more efficiently to reduce mishaps and wasted time.

- Reduce stress associated with traveling.

- Make the most of time on the road.

The key to effective business travel is to make only those trips you have to make. Always ask if a business trip is necessary. Can someone else go in your place? Can the business be handled with a conference call or virtual meeting? If you absolutely must take a business trip, success depends on effective planning.

BECOMING A TIME-SAVVY TRAVELER (10 MINUTES)

 Facilitator: Distribute Handout 9.1: Checklist for Becoming a Time-Savvy Traveler.

The first step for a successful trip occurs long before you leave home. Determine your goals for the trip and decide whom you need to meet with, when you need to meet, and where you have to go. Arrange appointments and meetings so that you can move easily from one to the next. This is especially important if you have to travel in unfamiliar locations. If you have an administrative assistant or secretary, get him involved early, and let him handle the actual arrangements.

Create a folder for each appointment, meeting, and location and begin to file everything you need in those folders. Consult with a travel agent or your company's travel department to create an itinerary that maximizes your time and minimizes your stress.

When you book your flight, allow plenty of time for travel to and from the airport. Plan for delays. Security clearances can jam up check-in, so make allowances.

Question: What is the best flight of the day? Ask for responses.

Answer: The first flight out is the best flight of the day since it is least likely to be delayed or canceled. Always have an alternate plan if your flight is delayed or canceled.

CHECKLIST FOR BECOMING A TIME-SAVVY TRAVELER

❏ Ask if this trip is necessary.

❏ Set goals for your trip.

❏ Create folders for meetings and locations.

❏ Create an itinerary that maximizes your time and minimizes your stress.

❏ Plan for delays and canceled flights.

❏ Find out what business amenities hotels offer.

❏ Join preferred flyer and hotel guest clubs.

❏ Book ground transportation.

❏ Obtain maps.

❏ Leave copies of your itinerary with your family and office.

❏ Create a Master List for ease of packing.

❏ Call the airline before leaving home to find out if your flight is on time.

❏ Check in according to the requirements of your airline.

❏ Double-check destination tags for checked luggage.

❏ Place a distinctive identification tag on your luggage.

❏ Bring something to occupy your time.

Get your seat assignment when you book the flight, if you can, to ensure that you get the location and type of seat you want. If you can upgrade to business or first class, do so.

Window seats are good if you plan on working during the trip. Aisle seats are good for quick getaways when you land. Mothers with small children tend to book the bulkhead seats, so you might want to avoid sitting there. Emergency exit aisles usually offer more legroom. If you meet the qualifications for handling the emergency doors, ask for these seats.

If you need assistance, such as a golf cart or wheelchair, arrange for it ahead of time. Airlines are restricting the size and amount of carry-ons, so check with your carrier about restrictions when you book your flight.

When you book your hotel accommodations, find out what business amenities are offered. Are rooms modem-ready? Is there a business center? Can you send and receive faxes in your room?

You can save a lot of time by using the same hotel chain for all business travel and joining its preferred guest club. Preferred status gives you many time-saving perks, such as express check-in and check-out, free daily newspapers, and use of concierge suites for breakfast and afternoon cocktails.

Decide what form of ground transportation you want to use—car rental, shuttles, buses, etc. Make sure you book these when you book your flight. If you plan on driving, obtain road maps before you leave. Online services can give you door-to-door directions, and you can buy software for your laptop that will give you driving directions while you're on the road.

Finalize your itinerary, and leave copies with your family and at the office. Make sure you include names, locations, and phone numbers for all meetings, a list of hotels where you will be staying, and the car rental agencies you are using.

Group Discussion

What are some other tips for better business traveling? Lead a group discussion.

 Facilitator: Add to the checklist in Handout 9.1. You will find that many participants have excellent suggestions. Be sure to add particularly good suggestions to your master list so you can share them with future participants.

CREATING A MASTER LIST (10 MINUTES)

 Facilitator: Distribute Handout 9.2: Travel Master List.

TRAVEL MASTER LIST

Outerwear	Undergarments
Toiletries	Equipment
Medical Kit	Supplies
Travel Documents	Sleepwear
Accessories	Business Documents and Materials
Reading Material	Other

Commentary

If you travel a lot, you need a master list of items to be packed for a one-night, two-night, and three-night trip. You are going to work with your team and draw up your personal master list of items that are essential for traveling.

As you can see, the worksheet is broken down by categories. Here are some examples of items to get you started:

- *Outerwear* includes the business and/or casual attire you will need, including shoes and hosiery.

- *Undergarments* is pretty obvious. Women should not forget extra pantyhose or nylons in the right color for their outfit.

- *Toiletries* include cosmetics and things like deodorant and toothpaste.

- *Equipment* is a list of items such as alarm clocks, steamers, cameras, and computer.

- *Medical Kit* includes prescription drugs and eyeglasses.

- *Supplies* are items such as paper, pens, coffee, and tea.

- *Travel Documents* are tickets, passports, and items such as these.

- *Sleepwear* is obvious.

- *Accessories* are jewelry, belts, scarves, and so on.

- *Business Documents and Materials* includes overheads, diskettes, and reports.

- *Reading Material* includes magazines, books, and clippings you need to read.

Team Activity: Creating a Master List

Instructions to Participants: Working with your team, create your master list. You have ten minutes for this exercise.

Ask for questions.

Debriefing: Call the room to order and have one or two teams share their lists.

Keep your master list with your luggage.

Before heading for the airport, call to find out if your flight is on time. Make sure you check in and arrive at your gate according to your airline's instructions, or you could be bumped from your flight.

Join the airline's premier passenger club. Members can access special waiting rooms designed to make travel more convenient and travel time more productive.

Some people prefer to check luggage; others want to carry it on. You save time at your destination if you carry on luggage.

If you check luggage, remove old destination tags. Make sure you get a claim check for each piece and that the agent affixes the correct three-digit destination tag to your luggage.

Put a brightly colored, distinctive identification tag on all of your suitcases so you can easily spot them when they arrive at the baggage handling area. Double-check your name tag before walking away with luggage since suitcases can look alike.

Always bring something to occupy your time. Waiting in airports is prime time to edit documents, review or prepare reports, or catch up on reading. Take your "to-read" file, and set a goal to empty it by the time you arrive at your destination.

Ask for questions.

TIME MANAGEMENT STRATEGIES (15 MINUTES)

We've come to the end of our two-day time management program. Does anyone have any questions about any part of the program?

Open the room to questions and discussion.

Team Activity: Time Management Challenges

Look at the list of time management challenges you identified yesterday and worked on this morning. If there are any open items, work with your team to create strategies for them. You have ten minutes for this exercise. Ask for two to three teams to share their strategies.

 Show Overhead 9.3: Time Management Strategies.

Time Management Strategies

9.3

COURSE ASSESSMENT (10 MINUTES)

 Facilitator: Distribute Handout 9.3: Certificate of Achievement and Handout 9.4: Course Assessment.

 Show Overhead 9.4: Course Assessment.

Course Assessment

For each item on the list, check the box that corresponds to the number that you believe applies to the item.

1 = Strongly disagree
2 = Disagree
3 = Not sure
4 = Agree
5 = Strongly agree

9.4

CERTIFICATE OF ACHIEVEMENT

Instructor:

Title of program:

Date:

Location:

This certifies that _____ [name] has successfully completed the Time Management Workshop on _____ [date].

[Instructor's signature]

COURSE ASSESSMENT

Instructor:

Title of Program:

Date: Time:

Location:

For each item on the list, check the box that corresponds to the number that you believe applies to the item.

> 1 = Strongly disagree
> 2 = Disagree
> 3 = Not sure
> 4 = Agree
> 5 = Strongly agree

Item	1	2	3	4	5
I can apply the information from the workshop on my job.					
I can relate to the examples and problems in the workshop.					
I learned new skills to use on the job.					
I would recommend this workshop to other employees.					
Information was clearly communicated.					
Learning objectives for the workshop were clear.					
Learning objectives for the workshop were met.					
The handouts made it easier to apply the information to my job.					
The handouts were easy to use.					
The instructor was organized and efficient.					
The instructor encouraged participation.					
The instructor handled group discussions well.					
The instructor handled questions well.					
The instructor kept my interest.					

Item	1	2	3	4	5
The instructor knew the material.					
The instructor maintained control of the class.					
The instructor used examples I could relate to.					
The instructor used overheads effectively.					
The instructor was well prepared.					
The instructor's delivery was lively and interesting.					
The length of the workshop was about right.					
The modules were presented in a logical manner.					
The overheads added to the presentation.					
The overheads made it easier to understand the material.					
The pace of the workshop was appropriate.					
The individual exercises helped me apply the information to my job.					
The room was comfortable.					
The team activities were valuable.					
The workshop was fun.					

I believe that the workshop could be improved in the following way(s):

I liked these aspects of the workshop:

Before we adjourn, please take a few minutes to complete this course assessment. Your input is very important. We will use it to decide how the workshop can be improved to better meet your needs.

You can leave your assessment at your place and I will collect them later. I'll be here for about another half-hour if anyone wants to chat about the workshop or has any additional questions.

I appreciate your attention and contributions over the past two days. You have helped make the workshop a success. If you think of anything that would improve the workshop after you return to your office, please let me know. You can reach me at [insert phone number and email address].

Again, thank you and good luck.

Managing Time on the Road—Notes

Review Module 8 Managing Time on the Road Objectives for Module 9	
Becoming a Time-Savvy Traveler	
Creating a Master List	
Time Management Strategies	
Course Assessment	

APPENDIX A

LIST OF OVERHEADS

Module 1

Module 2

Module 3

Overhead 3.1   Developing Concentration and Focus
Overhead 3.2   Objectives for Module 3
Overhead 3.3   When You Pay Attention
Overhead 3.4   Controlling Distractions
Overhead 3.5   Handling Interruptions
Overhead 3.6   Handling Interruptions (continued)
Overhead 3.7   Learning to Concentrate by Listening

Module 4

Overhead 4.1   Making Friends with Procrastination
Overhead 4.2   Objectives for Module 4
Overhead 4.3   Factors Contributing to Procrastination
Overhead 4.4   Fear and Procrastination
Overhead 4.5   Being Overwhelmed and Procrastination
Overhead 4.6   Setting Priorities
Overhead 4.7   Perfectionism and Procrastination
Overhead 4.8   Distaste and Procrastination
Overhead 4.9   Steps for Effective Delegation
Overhead 4.10 Avoiding Procrastination in the Future

Module 5

Overhead 5.1   Solving Productivity Challenges
Overhead 5.2   Understanding Work Styles
Overhead 5.3   Objectives for Module 5
Overhead 5.4   Larks and Owls
Overhead 5.5   Motivation Styles
Overhead 5.6   Work Styles

Module 6

Overhead 6.1   Mastering Meetings
Overhead 6.2   Objectives for Module 6
Overhead 6.3   Types of Meetings
Overhead 6.4   Creating Visual Aids and Handouts
Overhead 6.5   Meeting Leader Responsibilities
Overhead 6.6   Presenting with Power
Overhead 6.7   Stimulating Participation
Overhead 6.8   Reaching Decisions
Overhead 6.9   Handling Difficult People
Overhead 6.10 Managing Conflict and Confrontation
Overhead 6.11 Managing Conflict and Confrontation (continued)
Overhead 6.12 Attending a Meeting

Module 7

Overhead 7.1 Decision Making and Setting Priorities
Overhead 7.2 Objectives for Module 7
Overhead 7.3 Seven Steps to Effective Decision Making

Module 8

Overhead 8.1 Creating Balance and Setting Boundaries
Overhead 8.2 Objectives for Module 8
Overhead 8.3 Where Are You Out of Balance?
Overhead 8.4 Setting Priorities
Overhead 8.5 Priorities after "This-or-That" Process
Overhead 8.6 Setting SMART Goals
Overhead 8.7 Setting Boundaries

Module 9

Overhead 9.1 Managing Time on the Road
Overhead 9.2 Objectives for Module 9
Overhead 9.3 Time Management Strategies
Overhead 9.4 Course Assessment

Welcome to Time Management

0.1

Program Objectives

- Discover where your time goes.

- Reduce time wasters.

- Get organized.

- Build on your strengths.

- Work with others.

0.2

Program Objectives *(continued)*

- Develop focus.
- Make decisions and prioritize activities.
- Manage meetings.
- Make friends with procrastination.
- Create balance.

0.3

Time Management vs. Productivity

1.1

Objectives for Module 1

- Understand the difference between time management and productivity

- Identify how you currently spend time.

- Identify and eliminate time wasters.

- Create goals to support essential job functions.

- Plan to improve productivity.

The Value of Goals

You can:

- Measure progress.
- Reduce stress.
- Develop self-confidence.
- Become a star performer.

1.3

SMART Goals

Specific: Spell out each goal in detail.

Measurable: You need to evaluate success.

Adaptable: Goals need to respond to what's happening in your life.

Realistic: Blue sky, but be real!

Timely: Put a deadline on each goal.

The Benefits of Planning

Planning helps you:

- Anticipate challenges.

- Stay on target.

- Be more productive.

- Focus on critical activities.

- Gather needed resources.

- Identify effort and expense.

1.5

Getting Organized

2.1

Objectives for Module 2

- Understand and apply principles of organization.
- Understand filing strategies.
- Eliminate clutter.
- Create order.
- Organize your work space.

2.2

Principles of Organization

- Organize to support your goals.

- Designate a place for everything, and keep everything in its place.

- Honor your personal style.

2.3

Sort and Toss Session

- Create one or more piles
  - Act
  - Recycle or toss
    - File
    - Decide
    - Respond
    - Read

2.4

What to Keep

- Hard-to-replace items
- Legally required documents
- Documentation
- Originals

2.5

Filing Strategies

- Label files.
- Create a Master List.
- House based on frequency of use.
- Ensure confidentiality.

Sample File Categories

Insurance

Allstate

Liability Policies

Automobile Policies

Organizing Your Work Space

- Primary work space
- Secondary work space
- Functional and comfortable

2.8

Organize These Items

- Eliminate obsolete and duplicate documents.

- Refer documents.

- Create historical files.

- Update manuals.

- Cluster like things.

- File loose papers or house them in a binder.

2.9

Managing Phones

- Cluster phone activity.

- Make sure messages have complete information.

- Update voicemail message daily.

- Keep the phone area neat.

- Avoid telephone tag.

- Leave thorough voicemail messages.

- Program frequently used numbers.

Managing Email

- Send only simple documents.

- Do not send confidential information.

- Cluster email activity.

- Screen by sender's name and subject line.

- Be concise and professional.

Managing Computer Files and Software

- Label computer files.
- Archive old files.
- Label diskettes.
- Delete obsolete files and software.
- Back up daily.
- Learn how to save time with software.
- Make sure computer is positioned correctly.
- Take regular breaks.

2.12

Developing Concentration and Focus

3.1

Objectives for Module 3

- Focus energy and attention on what's important.

- Learn how to enter and use flow states.

- Identify, reduce, and eliminate distractions and interruptions.

3.2

When You Pay Attention

- Energy flows where attention goes.

- Now is the moment of power.

Controlling Distractions

- Visual
- Auditory
- Kinesthetic

3.4

Handling Interruptions

- Allow time in schedule.

- Identify patterns.

- Be assertive.

- Use wrap-up phrases.

- Handle phones.

- Schedule undisturbed time.

Handling Interruptions (continued)

- Be unavailable.

- Leave the office.

- Postpone routine matters.

- Use email and voicemail.

- Don't socialize.

- Politely ask visitors to leave.

- Don't interrupt others.

- Learn to concentrate.

3.6

Learning to Concentrate by Listening

Making Friends with Procrastination

4.1

Objectives for Module 4

- Understand and recognize contributing factors.

- Create strategies for working with procrastination.

4.2

Factors Contributing to Procrastination

- Fear
- Being overwhelmed
- Perfectionism
- Distaste

4.3

Fear and Procrastination

- Success breeds success.

- Assess likelihood of worst case.

- Use goals for motivation.

- Rehearse.

- Find role models.

4.4

Being Overwhelmed and Procrastination

- You have too much to do.

- You are facing a large, complex project.

4.5

Setting Priorities

- Does the activity contribute to goals?

- Who values this activity? How important is this person?

- What are the consequences of not doing it?

- Is there a deadline?

- Is the deadline within the next five working days?

4.6

Perfectionism and Procrastination

- Strive for accuracy, not perfection.

- Set small, easy-to-achieve goals.

- Use realistic standards.

- Forgive mistakes.

- Remember: "Good enough" is good enough.

4.7

Distaste and Procrastination

- Just do it.
- Delegate it.
- Swap.
- Don't do it.
- Postpone doing it.

4.8

Steps for Effective Delegation

1. Identify tasks that can be delegated.

2. Select the person.

3. Does he or she have the needed expertise?

4. Meet with the person to discuss the assignment.

5. Periodically obtain feedback.

6. Review results and evaluate how they measure up to expected results. Give the employee credit for a job well done.

Avoiding Procrastination in the Future

- Visualize the result.

- What are the benefits of doing it?

- What happens if you don't do it?

- Clear the clutter.

- Get information.

- Get help.

- Set small goals.

- Reward yourself.

Solving Productivity Challenges

- Discover where your time goes.

- Reduce time wasters.

- Get organized.

- Develop focus.

- Make friends with procrastination.

5.1

Understanding Work Styles

Objectives for Module 5

- Work with people who have differing styles.
- Understand how energy patterns affect productivity.
- Understand what motivates others.

Larks and Owls

Larks = Morning People

Owls = Evening People

5.4

Motivation Styles

- Toward/away from
- Internal/external
- Self/other

5.5

Work Styles

- Lark vs. Owl
- Toward vs. Away From
- Internal vs. External
- Self vs. Other

5.6

Mastering Meetings

6.1

Objectives for Module 6

- Communicate more effectively in groups.
- Reduce time in meetings.
- Create teamwork, consensus, and support.
- Accomplish more in less time.
- Improve the quality of meetings.

6.2

Types of Meetings

- Information meetings
- Decision-making meetings
- Regular meetings

6.3

Creating Visual Aids and Handouts

- Simple and easy to read

- Large typefaces and fewer than seven lines

- Use of talking points

- Use of clip art and color

- Respect for copyright protection

6.4

Meeting Leader Responsibilities

- Monitor content.

- Provide direction.

- Encourage interaction.

- Create atmosphere of cooperation.

- Move the meeting forward.

Presenting with Power

- Verbal skills
- Nonverbal skills

6.6

Stimulating Participation

- Brainstorming
- Brain drain
- Drawing people out

Reaching Decisions

- Define problem/situation.
- Recap information.
- Discuss options.
- Ask for a decision.
- Communicate decision.

Handling Difficult People

- Long-winded people
- Bulldozers
- Know-it-alls
- Sneaks
- Naysayers

6.9

Managing Conflict and Confrontation

- Don't take sides.

- Stop nonconstructive disputes.

- Stay calm and objective.

- Use "I" sentences.

Managing Conflict and Confrontation (continued)

- Ask questions.

- State outcomes.

- Resolve the conflict or table the discussion.

- Take a break.

6.11

Attending a Meeting

- Do you have to attend?
- Enter the meeting on your calendar.
- Ask for an agenda.
- Gather information.
- Prepare.
- Offer to take minutes.
- Keep the meeting on track.

6.12

Decision Making and Setting Priorities

7.1

Objectives for Module 7

- Understand the decision-making process.

- Learn strategies for making decisions more quickly and confidently.

- Take calculated risks.

- Identify and evaluate alternatives and relative risks.

7.2

Seven Steps to Effective Decision Making

1. Defining the goal
2. Gathering facts and information
3. Developing potential options
4. Evaluating options
5. Selecting an option
6. Implementing your decision
7. Evaluating your decision

© 2001 Patricia Haddock.

7.3

Creating Balance and Setting Boundaries

Objectives for Module 8

- Evaluate satisfaction with different areas of your life.

- Identify stressors.

- Create strategies for more balance.

- Create a benchmark for progress.

- Establish boundaries.

8.2

Where Are You Out of Balance?

- Career/Work
- Relationships/Romance
- Money Matters
- Health and Wellness
- Family/Friends
- Physical Environment
- Recreation/Rejuvenation
- Spiritual
- Personal Growth

8.3

Setting Priorities

A. Career/Work

B. Money Matters

C. Family/Friends

D. Physical Environment

E. Health and Wellness

8.4

Priorities after "This-or-That" Process

1. Money Matters

2. Physical Environment

3. Family/Friends

4. Health and Wellness

5. Career/Work

Setting SMART Goals

- **S**pecific: Spell out each goal in detail.

- **M**easurable: You need to evaluate success.

- **A**daptable: Goals need to respond to what's happening in your life.

- **R**ealistic: Blue sky, but be real!

- **T**imely: Put a deadline on each goal.

Setting Boundaries

- Communicate.

- Learn to say "no."

- Be treated fairly and with honesty.

- Require respect.

- Refer to your top three priorities and goals.

- Be flexible and respond to the moment.

8.7

Managing Time on the Road

9.1

Objectives for Module 9

- Reduce mishaps and wasted time.

- Reduce stress.

- Make the most of time on the road.

9.2

Time Management Strategies

9.3

Course Assessment

For each item on the list, check the box that corresponds to the number that you believe applies to the item.

1 = Strongly disagree

2 = Disagree

3 = Not sure

4 = Agree

5 = Strongly agree

9.4

APPENDIX B

LIST OF HANDOUTS

Background and Preparation

Workshop Checklist
Participant Roster
Certificate of Achievement
Course Assessment

Module 1

Handout 1.1	Sample Time Log
Handout 1.2	Time Log
Handout 1.3	Identifying Time Wasters
Handout 1.4	Doing What's Most Important
Handout 1.5	Setting SMART Goals
Handout 1.5a	Sample Set of SMART Goals
Handout 1.6	Planning to Reach Your Goals

Module 2

Handout 2.1	Review Module 1
Handout 2.2	Setting Organization Goals
Handout 2.3	Sort and Toss Checklist
Handout 2.4	Checklist for Filing Success
Handout 2.5	Setting Up Files
Handout 2.6	How Do You Handle These Environmental Challenges?
Handout 2.7	Organize These Items
Handout 2.8	Telephone Dos and Don'ts
Handout 2.9	Email Dos and Don'ts
Handout 2.10	Checklist for Managing Computer Files and Software

Module 3

Handout 3.1   Organization Obstacles and Solutions
Handout 3.2   Your Concentration Quotient
Handout 3.3   Where Does Your Concentration Go?
Handout 3.4   Controlling Your Environment
Handout 3.5   Interruption Action Plan
Handout 3.6   Checklist for Listening Skills

Module 4

Handout 4.1   Eliminating Workplace Distractions
Handout 4.2   What Is Your Procrastination Pattern?
Handout 4.3   Remembering Your Past Successes
Handout 4.4   What Does Success Mean to You?
Handout 4.5   Steps for Effective Delegation
Handout 4.6   Avoiding Procrastination in the Future

Module 5

Handout 5.1   Solving Productivity Challenges
Handout 5.2   Checklist for Larks and Owls
Handout 5.3   What's Your Motivation Style?
Handout 5.4   Working with Other People

Module 6

Handout 6.1   The Top 10
Handout 6.2   Meeting Planner Worksheet
Handout 6.3   Sample Agenda
Handout 6.4a   Sample Small Meeting Room Setup
Handout 6.4b   Sample Small to Moderate Meeting Room Setup
Handout 6.4c   Sample Large Meeting Room Setup
Handout 6.5   Rating Yourself as a Meeting Leader
Handout 6.6   Reading Body Language
Handout 6.7   Solutions to Reading Body Language
Handout 6.8   How Would You Manage This Meeting Challenge?
Handout 6.9   Meeting Evaluation
Handout 6.10   Checklist for Attending a Meeting

Module 7

Handout 7.1   Seven Steps to More Effective Decision Making
Handout 7.2   Checklist for Evaluating Options
Handout 7.3   What Do You Do?

Module 8

Module 9

WORKSHOP CHECKLIST

Instructor:

Title of program:

Date: Time:

Location:

Number of participants:

Location of facilities, i.e., cafeteria, coffee shop, bathrooms, etc.:

Room arrangement: ___ classroom ___ auditorium ___ U-shaped

Check the following materials as needed:

	Need	Obtained
Meeting room	_____	_____
Tables and chairs		
Quantities: Tables	_____	_____
Chairs	_____	_____
Breakout rooms	_____	_____
Tables for supplies/materials/etc.	_____	_____
Overhead projector and screen	_____	_____
Overhead transparencies	_____	_____
LCD projector and screen	_____	_____
Computer	_____	_____
Flipchart and markers	_____	_____
Whiteboard and markers	_____	_____
Slide projector	_____	_____
Video equipment	_____	_____
Audio equipment	_____	_____

Handheld microphone   _____   _____

Lapel microphone   _____   _____

A/V technical support   _____   _____

Water and glasses   _____   _____

Refreshments   _____   _____

    Coffee   _____   _____

    Tea   _____   _____

    Soft drinks   _____   _____

    Juice   _____   _____

    Breakfast   _____   _____

    Lunch   _____   _____

    Snacks   _____   _____

Handouts   _____   _____

Masking tape   _____   _____

Writing materials   _____   _____

    Paper   _____   _____

    Pens   _____   _____

Notepads/unlined paper   _____   _____

Tent card/name tags   _____   _____

PARTICIPANT ROSTER

Instructor:

Title of program:

Date: Time:

Location:

Participant Name	Department	Phone Number	Email Address

CERTIFICATE OF ACHIEVEMENT

Instructor:

Title of program:

Date:

Location:

This certifies that _____ [name] has successfully completed the Time Management Workshop on _____ [date].

[Instructor's signature]

COURSE ASSESSMENT

Instructor:

Title of program:

Date: Time:

Location:

For each item below, check the box that corresponds to the number that you believe applies to the item.

1 = Strongly disagree
2 = Disagree
3 = Not sure
4 = Agree
5 = Strongly agree

Item	1	2	3	4	5
I can apply the information from the workshop on my job.					
I can relate to the examples and problems in the workshop.					
I learned new skills to use on the job.					
I would recommend this workshop to other employees.					
Information was clearly communicated.					
Learning objectives for the workshop were clear.					
Learning objectives for the workshop were met.					
The handouts made it easier to apply the information to my job.					
The handouts were easy to use.					
The instructor was organized and efficient.					
The instructor encouraged participation.					
The instructor handled group discussions well.					
The instructor handled questions well.					
The instructor kept my interest.					
The instructor knew the material.					

The instructor maintained control of the class.					
The instructor used examples I could relate to.					
The instructor used overheads effectively.					
The instructor was well prepared.					
The instructor's delivery was lively and interesting.					
The length of the workshop was about right.					
The modules were presented in a logical manner.					
The overheads added to the presentation.					
The overheads made it easier to understand the material.					
The pace of the workshop was appropriate.					
The individual exercises helped me apply the information to my job.					
The room was comfortable.					
The team activities were valuable.					
The workshop was fun.					

I believe that the workshop could be improved in the following way(s):

I liked these aspects of the workshop:

SAMPLE TIME LOG

Instructions: List each activity you do for two weeks to find out where your time goes. Enter the date, a brief description of the activity, the time you began and ended it, and a ranking for its importance. Rank an activity from 5 to 1, with 5 for the activities critical to your success and 1 for activities that contribute little to your success. Keep your log for at least two weeks. At the end of the two weeks, analyze the log to see where your time goes and develop strategies for streamlining activities, eliminating time wasters, and becoming more productive.

Date	Activity	Time Started/Ended	Rank
8/9	Up/shower/breakfast	5:30 A.M./5:45 A.M.	N/A
	Commute	5:45 A.M./6:45 A.M.	N/A
	Breakfast meeting with clients	6:45 A.M./7:30 A.M.	4
	Travel to office	7:30 A.M./8:00 A.M.	N/A
	Returned emails	8:00 A.M./8:35 A.M.	3
	Retrieved voicemails	8:35 A.M./8:45 A.M.	3
	Returned voicemails	8:45 A.M./9:25 A.M.	3
	Began writing ABC proposal	9:25 A.M./10:20 A.M.	4
	Answered phone call	10:20 A.M./10:25 A.M.	2
	Interrupted by employee with questions about procedures	10:25 A.M./10:40 A.M.	2
	Continued writing ABC proposal	10:40 A.M./12:05 P.M.	4
	Lunch	12:05 P.M./1:15 P.M.	N/A
	Returned emails	1:15 P.M./1:35 P.M.	3
	Retrieved voicemails	1:35 P.M./1:45 P.M.	3
	Returned voicemails	1:45 P.M./2:25 P.M.	3
	Meeting on new marketing project	2:30 P.M./4:45 P.M.	4
	Returned emails	4:50 P.M./5:00 P.M.	3
	Retrieved voicemails	5:00 P.M./5:10 P.M.	3
	Returned voicemails	5:10 P.M./5:35 P.M.	3
	Commute	5:45 P.M./7:15 P.M.	N/A

	Exercise	7:15 P.M./8:00 P.M.	4
	Dinner/family time	8:00 P.M./9:30 P.M.	5
	Work on monthly report	9:30 P.M./10:45 P.M.	3
	Time Log evaluation	10:45 P.M./11:00 P.M.	N/A
	Bed	11:00 P.M.	N/A

Time Log Evaluation

- How satisfied are you with your day? *Moderately*
- How much time did you spend on the most important activities (those you rated 4s or 5s)? *7.5 hours*
- How much time did you spend on less important activities? *4.75 hours*
- Was your day balanced? *Pretty much*
- Did you take action on your most important goals? *Yes*

TIME LOG

Instructions: List each activity you do for two weeks to find out where your time goes. Enter the date, a brief description of the activity, the time you began and ended it, and a ranking for its importance. Rank an activity from 5 to 1, with 5 for activities critical to your success and 1 for activities that contribute little to your success. Keep your log for at least two weeks. At the end of the two weeks, analyze the log to see where your time goes and develop strategies for streamlining activities, eliminating time wasters, and becoming more productive.

Date	Activity	Time Started/Ended	Rank

Time Log Evaluation

- How satisfied are you with your day?
- How much time did you spend on the most important activities?
- How much time did you spend on less important activities?
- Was your day balanced?
- Did you take action on your most important goals?

IDENTIFYING TIME WASTERS

Instructions: Choose three of these time wasters—or some of your own—and working with your team, create three strategies for reducing or eliminating them.

1. How can I find files/papers faster?
2. How can I use voicemail to get things done?
3. How can I make decisions more quickly?
4. How can I get people to follow instructions better?
5. How can I meet deadlines more often?
6. How can I make my work space more efficient?
7. How can I better prioritize tasks?
8. How can I make myself throw out things I don't use and no longer need?
9. How can I handle my mail?
10. How can I make sure people call me back?
11. How can I get to the bottom of my in-box every day?
12. Other:

DOING WHAT'S MOST IMPORTANT

Instructions: Identify your top three career goals. What must you accomplish in order to ensure your success? Prioritize your goals from most important to least important. While all of these goals are important, establishing priorities will help you make better decisions and set smaller goals to accomplish what's most important.

Goal	Priority
1.	
2.	
3.	

SETTING SMART GOALS

Instructions: Take your top-priority goal and define three key smaller goals—a long-term goal to be met within the next three to five years; a mid-term goal to be met within the next one to three years, and a short-term goal to be met within the next twelve months. (Transfer each goal in the short-term column to Handout 1.6: Planning to Reach Your Goals.) Break each goal down into smaller SMART goals until you end up with a to-do list of activities and tasks.

Top-Priority Goal:

Long-Term Goal (3–5 years)	Mid-Term Goal (1–3 years)	Short-Term Goal (12 months)

- Is each goal SMART?
- What resources/training/help do you need to achieve this goal?
- Is this the right goal, or will another goal take you toward your objective faster and more easily?

SAMPLE SET OF SMART GOALS

Let's say that one of your top-priority goals is to start your own business in four years. Here's how your chart would look.

Top-Priority Goal: Start your own business

Long-Term Goal (3–5 years)	Mid-Term Goal (1–3 years)	Short-Term Goal (12 months)
Get my MBA in entrepreneurship.	Start program one year from now.	Research MBA programs within the next 6 weeks. Obtain information about likely programs within the next 3 months. Apply to likely programs within the next 6 months.

Transfer each goal in the Short-Term Goal column to Handout 1.6: Planning to Reach Your Goals and create smaller and smaller action steps.

PLANNING TO REACH YOUR GOALS

Instructions: Take your top-priority short-term goal from Handout 1.5 and write it here. Identify all the action steps that need to be taken to reach this goal.

Top-Priority Short-Term Goal:

Action Steps	Time Required	Deadline	Resources Needed

REVIEW MODULE 1

Instructions: Determine the three most important things you learned from Module 1: Time Management and Productivity. Commit to three action items to improve productivity when you return to your desk.

Most important things learned in Module 1:

1. _____

2. _____

3. _____

Action items to improve productivity:

1. _____

2. _____

3. _____

SETTING ORGANIZATION GOALS

Instructions: Identify your top three organization goals and rank them from most important to least important.

Objective	Priority
1.	
2.	
3.	

SORT AND TOSS CHECKLIST

☐ Create piles of everything that doesn't have a place or isn't in its place.

☐ Go through each pile from top to bottom, touching each piece of paper once, and ask these questions:

☐ Do you need to take action? If so, act now.

☐ Do you need this piece of paper again? If you don't need it, recycle it or toss it. If you do need it, where will you file it? Do you already have a file set up for it? If so, immediately file it away. If not, put it in a pile labeled "To Set Up Files."

☐ Can you make a decision now, or do you need more information? If you can make a decision, do so. If you need more information, where will you file this paper before you make a decision? How will you get the information you need?

☐ Do you need to respond? If so, how and when will you respond?

☐ Do you need to read this? Is this information still relevant? If it is more than six months old, consider tossing it. Store things you need to read in a "to-read" file, sorted by oldest to most current, and carry it with you. Make it a habit to read required information when you are waiting for a meeting to begin, on public transportation, and in small pockets of time that are too small to tackle a major project.

CHECKLIST FOR FILING SUCCESS

❏ Create files using broad headings with subcategories. You can label according to subject, alphabetically, geographically, chronologically, or numerically.

❏ Create a Master List with cross-references.

❏ Keep files you use frequently near your work area, and archive files you rarely use.

❏ Periodically conduct a Sort and Toss Session for each file drawer.

❏ Keep personnel files confidential, with access restricted to authorized people only. Medical information about employees must be filed apart from employment files and be kept confidential with access restricted to authorized people only.

❏ Stop accumulating paper. Use these tips to cut out paper:
  - Use the phone, electronic files, and email whenever possible.
  - Never put down a piece of paper without doing something to move it along.
  - Create files only as needed using the criteria established in this section.
  - Send copies to only those people who really need them.
  - Set up a place for incoming mail and paper. Empty this in-basket daily using the sort and toss method.
  - Set up a place for outgoing mail and paper.
  - Set up a "to-file" box and empty it daily.
  - Return files to their drawers promptly.
  - Label storage boxes for each identification and retrieval.

SETTING UP FILES

Set up files for these items, and identify major and subcategories of files for each:

- An invoice from Fred's Software Store for Office 2000
- An invoice from WaterWorks for bottled water
- A clipping from a newspaper about the growth of The Community Bank, one of your customers
- A magazine interview with your CEO, Jan Carson, about Widget 2010, which your company just introduced
- A signed contract for a vendor, Madison Temp, to provide temporary agency staff
- An employment application for Cathy Morris, who was hired for a sales job
- A letter of complaint about a defective widget from a customer, Wilson Winkler
- A stack of correspondence about an ongoing project to introduce Widget 3000
- Meeting records from the monthly staff meeting
- A brochure about an upcoming team-building workshop the CEO wants key people to attend

HOW DO YOU HANDLE THESE ENVIRONMENTAL CHALLENGES?

- A work space near the coffee room with heavy traffic all day
- A work space that makes you appear to be the office receptionist
- A work space near the mail room with constant activity, deliveries, and noise
- A work space near a bank of filing cabinets used by the entire department
- A poorly ventilated work space
- A poorly lit work space
- A work space with too much furniture

ORGANIZE THESE ITEMS

Item	How will you organize it?
Catalogs from office supply company for 1993, 1996, 1999, 2000	
Training manuals for three workshops: business writing, time management, and customer service	
Invoices from three vendors: office supplies, water delivery, and software products	
Company annual reports for past five years	
Brochures for upcoming workshops and seminars	
Telephone lists	
Meeting records for three projects: installation of new software, new customer service standards, and new product introduction	
Magazine articles on diversity, customer complaints, and sales tips	
Leads for new business	
Twenty-five business cards	
Invitation to a retirement dinner for a coworker	
New procedures for using company credit cards and handling incoming telephone calls	
Information about the company's health care and 401(k) plans	
Notes from three classes you recently attended: stress management, time management, and selling skills	
Information on the department's computer network	

Item	How will you organize it?
Paper clips, Post-it® Notes, staples, stapler, Liquid Paper, telephone, pictures of kids, pictures of cats, cartoon, pens, pencils, scissors, notebooks, dictionary, style manual, ruler, erasers, highlighters, desk lamp, clock, stuffed cow, ceramic cow	
Diskettes—blank and used	
Telephone directory	
List of phone usage for past three months	
Unsigned vendor contracts	

TELEPHONE DOS AND DON'TS

Dos

- Speak clearly and enunciate every word precisely.
- Speak more slowly than you would if you were meeting in person since it takes people longer to process auditory messages.
- Keep your greeting brief. Identify yourself and your reason for calling.
- Always leave your phone number. Don't make the other person look it up.
- Sound friendly and professional.
- Make friends with secretaries, administrative assistants, and receptionists.
- Ask permission before putting someone on hold, and explain why it is necessary. Thank her when you return to the phone.
- Focus your attention on the other person.
- Ask the person if this is a good time to talk.
- Plan what you want to accomplish with the call.
- Leave a message that states times when you can be reached by phone.

Don'ts

- Record long, cutesy voicemail messages or greetings that sound unprofessional.
- Put people on hold indefinitely.
- Carry on side conversations while you are on the phone.
- Allow interruptions while you are on the phone.
- Type on your computer keyboard while you are on the phone.
- Read your email while you are on the phone.
- Deliver a canned greeting.
- Persist if the person gives you a firm "no."
- Play telephone tag.
- Speed up when you leave your phone number.

EMAIL DOS AND DON'TS

Dos Receiving Email

- Check email regularly.
- Establish reading priorities based on subject and sender.
- Respond promptly.
- Be polite.
- Save emails you need for documentation.

Dos Sending Email

- Prepare what you want to say ahead of time.
- Be brief.
- Use descriptive subject lines.
- Be polite.
- Tell the recipient what action you want him to take early in the email.
- When replying, check to see who is getting your reply and edit the list, if necessary.
- Save emails you need for documentation.
- Regularly delete old email.

Don'ts Sending Email

- Ramble.
- Respond if you are angry or feeling any strong emotion.
- Flame—use all caps or exclamation marks.
- Be terse or abrupt.
- Give commands.
- Assume your email will be read.
- Send confidential messages.
- Send more than one attachment with each message.

Don'ts Receiving Email

- Open or respond to emails or download files from strangers.
- Save emails unless you need them for documentation.
- Forward jokes unless you know the recipient wants them.

CHECKLIST FOR MANAGING COMPUTER FILES AND SOFTWARE

❏ Set up and label computer files using the same system you use for paper files.

❏ File off old files to an archive diskette.

❏ Label diskettes so you can find files.

❏ Delete old drafts of completed projects, working drafts of documents, and, if appropriate, software you don't use.

❏ Back up your files at least once daily.

❏ If appropriate, carry key files with you on diskettes.

❏ To save time when using software:

- Create templates for frequently used documents and macros for frequently used phrases.
- Learn how to use software efficiently.
- Use shortcuts and commands.

❏ Make sure your computer is positioned for comfort and doesn't strain your vision or posture.

❏ Take a five-minute break every hour. Look away from your monitor, stand, and stretch.

ORGANIZATION OBSTACLES AND SOLUTIONS

Instructions: Place a check mark by the statements that apply to you.

___ I don't have time to get organized.

___ I don't know where to begin.

___ I have a hard time finding anything on my desk.

___ I haven't filed in more than a week.

___ My in-basket is always overflowing.

___ I have stacks of papers on the floor.

___ I have unread magazines that are more than one month old.

___ I have Post-it® Notes all over my desk and computer.

___ I don't have/use a calendar system.

___ I hate to throw anything away.

___ I spend a lot of time looking for stuff.

___ I don't remember where I have filed papers.

___ No one can help me organize my stuff.

___ I have business cards everywhere.

___ Things pop out of my drawers when I open them.

___ I have a lot of equipment and/or personal items on my desk.

___ I have very little room on my desktop to work.

___ I have lots of files with very few papers in each file folder.

Choose one of the items you checked and, working with your team, brainstorm solutions to eliminate it.

YOUR CONCENTRATION QUOTIENT

	Strongly Disagree	Disagree	Agree	Strongly Agree
People frequently interrupt me.				
When I am interrupted, it's hard to return my attention to the task at hand.				
When people interrupt me, I am reluctant to cut them off so I can go back to work.				
My attention wanders frequently.				
I find it difficult to concentrate.				
I often ask people to repeat what they say.				
I daydream a lot.				
I often feel frustrated at the end of the day because I haven't accomplished anything.				
I often feel scattered and ineffective.				
My office/cubicle makes people feel comfortable when they visit.				

WHERE DOES YOUR CONCENTRATION GO?

Instructions: Where does your concentration go? For the next two minutes, list everything you notice around you. What do you see? Hear? Touch or feel? Taste or smell? Note everything without stopping for two minutes.

Sight	Hearing
Touch or Feel	**Smell/Taste**

List here three steps you will take to make your work environment less distracting:

1. _____

2. _____

3. _____

CONTROLLING YOUR ENVIRONMENT

Instructions: Identify the environmental obstacles that prevent you from developing concentration and focus. Work with your team to come up with one strategy for eliminating or reducing the negative impact of this obstacle. You have ten minutes for this exercise.

- Inadequate lighting
- Uncomfortable chair and/or desk
- Clutter
- Noisy neighbors and/or equipment
- Ringing phones
- Visitors
- Being situated in a high-traffic area
- Background noise
- Poor airflow
- Temperature too hot/too cold
- Other:

INTERRUPTION ACTION PLAN

Instructions: The Boy Scout motto, "Be prepared," is good advice. Don't wait until you are trying to finish a report on deadline to figure out how you are going to handle interruptions. Start now to identify, reduce, and eliminate sources of interruptions.

The most common interruptions I cope with are:

_____

_____

_____

I will implement the following strategies for eliminating these interruptions in the future:

_____

_____

_____

CHECKLIST FOR LISTENING SKILLS

- ❏ Let people finish speaking before responding.
- ❏ Stay present.
- ❏ Demonstrate that you are paying attention.
- ❏ Pay attention to body language.
- ❏ Establish rapport.
- ❏ Control the conversation.
- ❏ Concentrate on facts and behaviors.
- ❏ Use silence.

ELIMINATING WORKPLACE DISTRACTIONS

Instructions: Review your answers to the exercise from Handout 3.3: Where Does Your Concentration Go? This exercise tells you where distractions are most likely to come from for you—whether they are visual, auditory, or kinesthetic. Work with your team to develop one strategy you can implement to help you eliminate or reduce this type of distraction. For example, if most of your distractions are visual and your desk faces a window, you may want to turn it so that it faces a wall. Or if you are auditory and your phone distracts you, you may want to turn off the ringer for part of each day so you can concentrate on important activity. You have fifteen minutes for this exercise.

_____

_____

_____

_____

_____

_____

WHAT IS YOUR PROCRASTINATION PATTERN?

Instructions: What situations cause you to procrastinate? In Column 1, describe the situations or activities where you procrastinate. Then, in Column 2, identify why you are procrastinating. You can use the list on this handout, or add your own reasons if they are not on the list.

Some reasons for procrastinating:

- Anxiety
- Boredom
- Fear of failure
- Fear of success
- Feelings of inadequacy
- Inexperience
- Lack of information
- Lack of interest
- Lack of organization
- Lack of relevance
- Lack of time
- Lack of training
- Not knowing where to start
- Perfectionism
- Performance fear
- Stress
- Other:

Situation Causing Procrastination	Why You Are Procrastinating
EXAMPLE: *Learning new skills*	*Fear of failure*

REMEMBERING YOUR PAST SUCCESSES

Instructions: List three obstacles from your past that you overcame. Your list can include more than just business endeavors. The more varied your list, the more you can draw on when you are procrastinating because of fear. State how you overcame your fear and include the strengths you drew upon to help you succeed.

Describe the obstacle you overcame	Describe how you overcame your fear
1.	1.
2.	2.
3.	3.

Refer to your list often and allow yourself to feel competent, accomplished, and successful as you review each achievement. Keep it handy for the tough times.

WHAT DOES SUCCESS MEAN TO YOU?

Instructions: Refer to Handout 1.4: Doing What's Most Important, Handout 1.5: Setting SMART Goals, and Handout 1.6: Planning to Reach Your Goals. Review the goals you set in Module 1. Working alone, identify what achieving your goals means to you. Check all that apply to you.

By reaching my goals, I can:

___ Have more freedom.

___ Be more creative.

___ Make more money.

___ Have more fun.

___ Do what's important to me.

___ Make a contribution.

___ Get a promotion.

___ Live my bliss.

___ Have more time for _____(fill in).

___ Other: _____

STEPS FOR EFFECTIVE DELEGATION

1. Identify tasks that can be delegated. Spend time on activities that only you can perform—activities that require your skills and knowledge and that contribute most to the achievement of your goals. Delegate tasks that require specialized skills to those with appropriate expertise.

2. Carefully select the person to whom you will delegate the task. Match tasks with skills while giving people the opportunity to stretch and grow.

3. Ask yourself if the employee has the expertise to succeed and if he can take on this assignment and meet your deadline.

4. Meet with the employee to discuss the assignment. Explain the nature of the assignment and what results you expect. Define any limits you want recognized, encourage questions, and give feedback. Make sure the employee understands how the task contributes to the success of your department/company.

5. Periodically obtain feedback from the employee. Provide coaching, if needed, but give people autonomy.

6. Review results and evaluate how they measure up to expected results. Give the employee credit for a job well done.

AVOIDING PROCRASTINATION IN THE FUTURE

This checklist shows some strategies you can employ to avoid procrastination in the future. You can add other strategies of your own.

- ❏ Visualize the result to the action steps you need to take.
- ❏ Write out the benefits of doing it.
- ❏ Write out what will happen if you don't do it or miss the deadline.
- ❏ Clear away clutter.
- ❏ Get the information you need.
- ❏ Get help if you need it.
- ❏ Set small, easily achieved goals.
- ❏ Reward yourself.

Work with your team to develop strategies for avoiding procrastination in the future using the situations and factors you identified in Handout 4.2: What Is Your Procrastination Pattern? For example, if you procrastinate when you face large projects, one strategy is to set small, easily achieved goals that you can work on for a set time each day.

SOLVING PRODUCTIVITY CHALLENGES

Productivity Challenge	Solutions

CHECKLIST FOR LARKS AND OWLS

❑ Schedule your day to maximize your peak energy hours.

❑ Set and adhere to a regular wake-up time.

❑ Get exposure to sunlight within fifteen minutes of awakening. Sunlight energizes your body and starts your internal clock ticking.

❑ If you feel your energy flagging during the day, go outside or find a window and stand or sit in sunlight for fifteen minutes.

❑ Schedule creative activities and activities that require intense concentration for times when your energy is high, usually the three or four hours after awakening.

❑ Exercise regularly.

❑ Take a catnap midway through the day.

❑ Schedule activities that require attention to detail for the hour before lunch.

❑ Schedule meetings for 11 A.M., when most people are alert and reasoning skills are good. Scheduling them just before lunch also means that you are more likely to end on time. Avoid meetings right after lunch.

❑ Eating protein helps raise alertness. Carbohydrates contribute to relaxation. Plan lunch and dinner based on what you need to do afterward. If you have an important meeting or presentation, order chicken or fish and avoid pasta. Avoid heavy, calorie-laden meals if you need to keep your energy up. The heavier the meal, the sleepier you will feel afterward.

❑ Do not skip meals. Hunger can adversely affect performance and create feelings of stress and anxiety.

❑ Schedule routine and/or repetitive activities for the hour right after lunch since your energy will be lowest at this time. Avoid activities that require accuracy or attention to detail.

❑ Just before heading home, plan the next day.

❑ Late afternoon is best for exercising since coordination is good at this time. Exercising later in the day also contributes to restfulness and a good night's sleep.

❑ A snack of carbohydrates before bedtime can induce sleepiness.

❑ Avoid alcohol and caffeine just before bedtime.

❑ Go to bed the same time every night to keep your internal clock on time.

WHAT'S YOUR MOTIVATION STYLE?

Instructions: Working alone, identify five achievements that you are proud of. They can be work-related or personal. Maybe you are proud of getting your driver's license at sixteen or graduating from college or getting a sports scholarship. Think about what motivated you to achieve these things. Did you learn how to drive because you wanted freedom or independence or because you didn't want your parents to drive you around? Did you graduate from college because you wanted to earn a degree or because your family expected you to get a degree? Identify your dominant motivation styles for each event and your overall pattern.

Event	Toward or Away From	Internal or External	Self or Other

My dominant motivation styles are:

WORKING WITH OTHER PEOPLE

Instructions: This handout describes the work styles of four different employees. Working with your team, decide how you will communicate with these employees to achieve the goals outlined in the exercise. Consider things such as the best time of day to meet with the people, the language you will use, and the arguments you will put forth to convince them to act in the way you want them to act.

Case Study 1: Sally is a lark, with a toward-internal-self style. How would you approach her to form and lead a team to plan the office United Way campaign?

_____

_____

Case Study 2: Henry is an owl with an away-from–external–other style. He has recently been promoted to your supervisor. How would you approach him to ask for a raise?

_____

_____

Case Study 3: Carlos is a lark with a toward-external-other style. How would you convince him to take a CPA class that would improve his chances for promotion?

_____

_____

Case Study 4: Janella is an owl with an away-from–internal–other style. How would you convince her to accept a lateral transfer to a new job with more responsibility but no additional pay?

_____

_____

THE TOP 10

Instructions: Working with your team, identify the Top 10 strategies you learned for working effectively with others. Then, each member of the team should choose three strategies to implement when you return to work.

1.

2.

3.

4.

5.

6.

7.

8.

9.

10.

Your three strategies:

1.

2.

3.

MEETING PLANNER WORKSHEET

1. What are your objectives for this meeting? Can the objectives be met without a meeting?

2. State specific measures you will use to evaluate the effectiveness of this meeting.

3. Set the date, time, and location for the meeting.

4. Identify participants who need to attend by using the following criteria:
   - What contribution will this person make?
   - Is it essential that this person attend in person?
   - Is this the best person to attend the meeting?
   - Can this person send a designee in his or her place?
   - Does this person have to be present for the entire meeting? Can he or she drop in and then leave?

5. Create and publish a meeting agenda that includes all of the following information:
   - Objectives for the meeting.
   - Date, time, and location, and directions to the meeting site, if necessary.
   - Discussion items, discussion leaders, and time frames for each discussion.
   - Breaks, if appropriate.

6. Invite participants.

7. Determine and see to the following:
   - Meeting room setup, i.e., conference room style, classroom style, lecture style, etc.
   - Electronic equipment, i.e., overhead projector, LCD screen, microphones, VCR, etc.
   - Materials, i.e., name tags, handout copies, notebooks, pencils, etc.
   - Refreshments, if appropriate

8. Leading the meeting:
   - Arrive early and ensure that the room is set up properly, electronic equipment is there and works, and materials are ready for distribution.
   - Greet participants as they arrive.
   - Begin on time.
   - State the objectives for the meeting.
   - Follow the agenda.

- Introduce each agenda item and the participant leading the discussion.
- Encourage participation.
- Allow time for discussions, and keep them on track.
- Provide summaries and feedback.
- Assign tasks and responsibilities for follow-up.

9. End the meeting on time.

10. Evaluate the effectiveness of the meeting based on measures defined.

11. Create and distribute meeting record with follow-up actions and tasks defined and assigned.

SAMPLE AGENDA

DATE: November 3, 2000

TIME: 9:15 A.M.–10:30 A.M.

LOCATION: Apollo Building, Conference Room 19-C
(19th floor, opposite the mail room)

OBJECTIVES:

- Help managers understand the new health care plan so they can explain it to their employees.
- Describe enrollment procedures.
- Provide materials for managers to give to employees.

Time	Topic	Person Responsible
9:15 A.M.	Start meeting	Ms. Connors
9:15 A.M.–9:30 A.M.	Introduce new plan	Ms. Barrows
9:30 A.M.–9:50 A.M.	Show videotape	Ms. Connors
9:50 A.M.–10:00 A.M.	Explain enrollment procedures	Ms. Connors
10:00 A.M.–10:15 A.M.	Questions	Ms. Barrows
10:30 A.M.	Conclude meeting	Ms. Barrows

Please confirm your attendance by October 30. If you cannot attend, please send someone to represent your unit.

SAMPLE SMALL MEETING ROOM SETUP

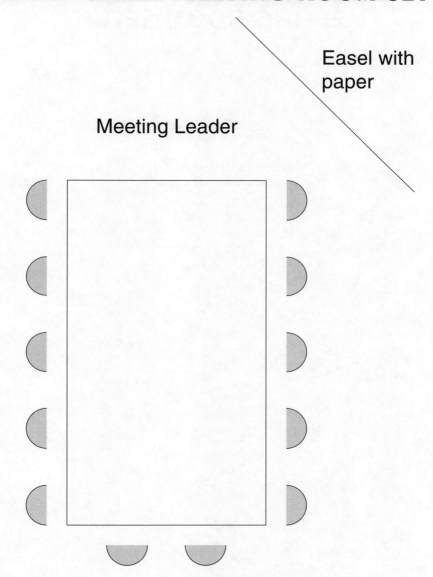

Easel with paper

Meeting Leader

Refreshments

SAMPLE SMALL TO MODERATE MEETING ROOM SETUP

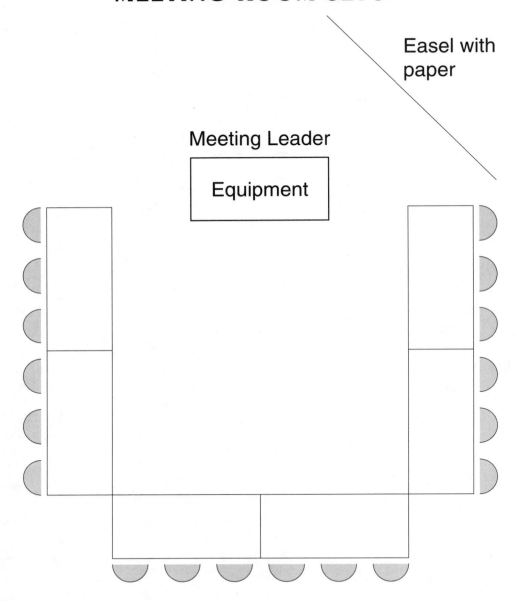

Easel with paper

Meeting Leader

Equipment

Refreshments

350

SAMPLE LARGE MEETING ROOM SETUP

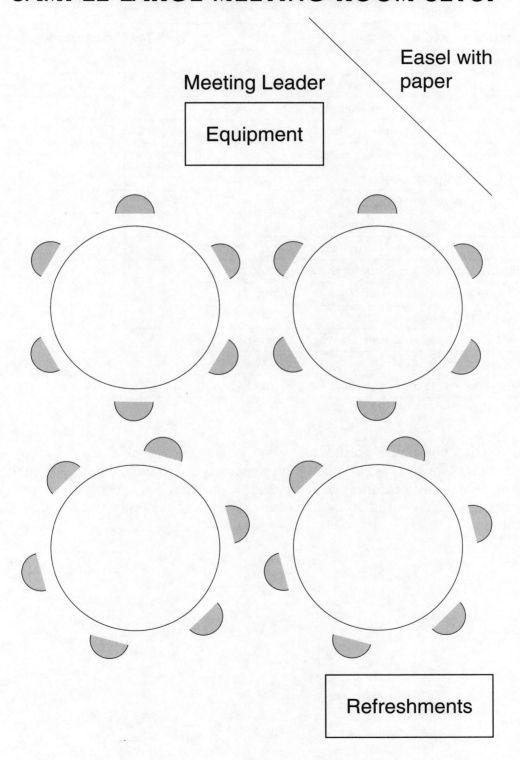

Meeting Leader

Easel with paper

Equipment

Refreshments

RATING YOURSELF AS A MEETING LEADER

When you lead a meeting . . .	Yes	Sometimes	No
The meeting begins on time.			
Everyone has a chance to express his or her opinion.			
I use an agenda to keep the meeting on track.			
The meeting ends on time.			
A meeting record is kept and published.			
Clear responsibility for follow-up actions is determined.			
A/V equipment works properly.			
Handouts contribute to the meeting objectives.			
I encourage fewer vocal participants to get involved.			
I resolve conflicts before they escalate.			
I require feedback from participants.			
I stimulate discussion.			
Overheads can be read from the back of the room.			
The agenda goes out ahead of the meeting.			
I keep assertive participants from controlling the meeting.			

Total _____

Score: Give yourself 5 points for every "Yes," 3 points for every "Sometimes," and 0 points for every "No." The higher your score, the stronger your meeting leader skills. Pay attention to every item you marked "Sometimes" or "No." These are areas where you can sharpen your meeting skills and become more productive.

READING BODY LANGUAGE

Instructions: Match the behavior described in the first column with the body language in the second column.

Behavior	Body Language
Steepled hands, hands behind back, hands in pockets	Openness
Open hands, unbuttoned jacket	Nervousness
Short breaths, clenched hands, wringing hands	Defensiveness
Pinching flesh, chewing gum, biting fingernails	Confidence
Arms crossed, rubbing nose and eyes, drawing away	Insecurity
Open hands, sitting on edge of chair, leaning forward	Frustration
Clearing throat, fidgeting, jiggling keys or money	Cooperation
Sitting/moving back, arms folded, head down	Engaged
Arms behind back, smiling, open stance	Listening
Head tilted, eye contact, nodding	Defiant
Closes papers, pen down, hands on table	Desire to speak
Hands on hips, frowning	Evaluating
Leaning forward, foot tapping, finger pointing	Desire to leave
Finger tapping, staring	Aggressive
Leaning forward, open body, open arms	Ready to agree
Sucks glasses/pen, looks right and left, crossed legs	Attentive
Feet toward door, looking around, buttoning jacket	Rejection

SOLUTIONS TO READING BODY LANGUAGE

Behavior	Body Language
A. Steepled hands, hands behind back, hands in pockets	Confidence
B. Open hands, unbuttoned jacket	Openness
C. Short breaths, clenched hands, wringing hands	Frustration
D. Pinching flesh, chewing gum, biting fingernails	Insecurity
E. Arms crossed, rubbing nose and eyes, drawing away	Defensiveness
F. Open hands, sitting on edge of chair, leaning forward	Cooperation
G. Clearing throat, fidgeting, jiggling keys or money	Nervousness
H. Sitting/moving back, arms folded, head down	Rejection
I. Arms behind back, smiling, open stance	Attentive
J. Head tilted, eye contact, nodding	Listening
K. Closes papers, pen down, hands on table	Ready to agree
L. Hands on hips, frowning	Defiant
M. Leaning forward, foot tapping, finger pointing	Aggressive
N. Finger tapping, staring	Desire to speak
O. Leaning forward, open body, open arms	Engaged
P. Sucks glasses/pen, looks right and left, crossed legs	Evaluating
Q. Feet toward door, looking around, buttoning jacket	Desire to leave

HOW WOULD YOU MANAGE THIS MEETING CHALLENGE?

Instructions: You are leading a meeting to introduce a new flexible time schedule for staff. Marge, a manager who is very critical of the new schedule, is constantly interrupting the speakers with negative comments and questions designed to challenge the speakers' expertise. You are starting to fall behind the agenda, and people are becoming restless and irritable. Some people are starting to agree with Marge's criticisms of the new schedule. One of your objectives for meeting is to gain the support of managers so the new schedule is positively positioned to employees. How will you handle this situation?

MEETING EVALUATION

Meeting:

Date: _____   Length:

Answer the following questions to evaluate the effectiveness of your meeting:

1. Were meeting objectives achieved?   Yes   No

2. Did the meeting begin on time?   Yes   No

3. Did the meeting end on time?   Yes   No

4. Did participants have a chance to express themselves?   Yes   No

5. Did participants seem satisfied with the meeting?   Yes   No

6. Were disputes resolved fairly?   Yes   No

7. Were participants encouraged to participate?   Yes   No

8. How can the meeting be improved?

CHECKLIST FOR ATTENDING A MEETING

What should you do when you are asked to attend a meeting?

☐ Find out if you have to attend in person. Can you send someone else? Do you have to attend the entire meeting, or can you attend the relevant part and then leave?

☐ Note the meeting on your calendar, and allow travel time. Make sure you include the location of the meeting and the name and phone number of your primary contact.

☐ Ask for an agenda to be sent to you before the meeting.

☐ Start a file for what you will need to take with you.

☐ If you are making a presentation, make sure you schedule time to prepare.

☐ Offer to take minutes. This gives you an excuse to keep things on track.

☐ If the meeting leader doesn't keep the meeting on track, gently move things along using statements such as "Can we discuss this offline?" "Before we move on, can we summarize where we are?" "I think we are off track. Can we return to the point we were pursuing?"

SEVEN STEPS TO MORE EFFECTIVE DECISION MAKING

1. Defining the goal
2. Gathering facts and information
3. Developing potential options
4. Evaluating options
5. Selecting an option
6. Implementing your decision
7. Evaluating your decision

CHECKLIST FOR EVALUATING OPTIONS

Each option represents a different course of action and a different decision. You need to ask and answer a series of questions about each option. In order to adequately answer these questions, you may need input from other people.

❏ What are the consequences of this option? Look for both long-term and short-term outcomes.

❏ How well does this option meet the goals you have identified? You may want to revisit your stated goal and decide if it is still the right goal or if you need to modify it.

❏ What effect does this option have on other people? How does the option affect other areas of your life or work?

❏ Is this option ethical? Does it reflect your values and those of your company? Would you feel comfortable if this option were to be made public knowledge?

❏ What are the trade-offs of this option? You need to understand clearly what you gain and lose with each option since it is unlikely that one option will be perfect.

❏ What are the risks associated with this option? How much risk can you handle? What could you potentially lose? Make sure you understand the worst-case scenario and are willing to accept it as a possibility.

❏ How much will the option cost in time, money, staff, resources, and so on? Relative costs are an important factor to consider.

❏ How does this option help you achieve better results? Does it help you achieve your goals faster?

❏ What is the likelihood of success for this option? How much uncertainty can you handle?

❏ Has the option been tried before? If so, what were the results? How is this situation similar? Different?

❏ How does this option affect future options? Does it expand or narrow future possibilities and potentialities?

❏ Other:

WHAT DO YOU DO?

Instructions: Working with your team, take the case study on the handout through the seven steps for decision making:

1. Define the goal.
2. You won't be able to gather facts and information, so just identify where and how you will get the information you need to make your decision. Assume that you have done your research.
3. Brainstorm potential options.
4. Create a list of pros and cons for two or three options.
5. Select an option.
6. Identify the action steps that need to be taken to implement your decision and who needs to be notified.
7. Create the criteria you will use to evaluate your decision.

Case Study:

Selena has been offered a promotion to a position in London. She will get a small salary increase and special compensation for an overseas assignment. The new position will take her career from administration to sales. She isn't sure she wants to make the shift since sales is a new area for her. She also isn't sure she wants to live overseas. What steps can Selena take to make a decision?

_____

_____

DECISION MAKING

Instructions: Working with your team, choose one of the following cases and decide how you will resolve the stalemate:

1. Hal is leading a team to implement a marketing campaign for a new software product. The success of the product hinges on the most effective campaign. ABC Marketing and Exeter Marketing have both responded to RFPs and are the final contenders. ABC has proposed an elaborate campaign that includes animation and high Web visibility. Exeter is taking a more moderate, traditional approach. Hal's team has been reviewing and discussing the proposals for three hours and needs to make a decision but is reluctant to commit. What steps can Hal take to help the team make a decision?

2. Mark and his partner, David, have been asked to design a Web site for a local nonprofit. Mark is eager to jump into the project since it will give the partners the chance to meet and work with several important businesspeople who could give them business. David is less eager because they currently have three major accounts to design Web sites for and are understaffed. Mark and David have been arguing for days. What steps can they take to come to a decision?

3. Steven, Pascal, Mary, Lassanda, and Hal work on a team to develop new customer service standards for their claims department. Steven and Pascal want to hold focus groups with phone contact people to get their input on the team's first draft of the new standards. Mary, Lassanda, and Hal think that no one should review the standards until management has had input. There are pluses and minuses for each approach. What steps can the team take to choose an approach?

LIFE BALANCE ASSESSMENT

Instructions: On a scale of 1 to 10, with 1 being totally unsatisfied and 10 being totally satisfied, rank how satisfied you are with the following areas of your life. In the box, write a brief description of this area as it is now.

For example:

Career/Work Rating: 4 Assessment: I have been working at night with my spouse in a restaurant he recently opened. My job is suffering because I am tired every day. I enjoy my job and have the opportunity for advancement. I also want to help my husband succeed. I feel torn and unsure of what to do.	1	2	3	4 X	5	6	7	8	9	10

Write your assessment and rating here.

Career/Work Rating: Assessment:	1	2	3	4	5	6	7	8	9	10

Relationships/Romance Rating: Assessment:	1	2	3	4	5	6	7	8	9	10
Money Matters Rating: Assessment:	1	2	3	4	5	6	7	8	9	10
Health and Wellness Rating: Assessment:	1	2	3	4	5	6	7	8	9	10
Family/Friends Rating: Assessment:	1	2	3	4	5	6	7	8	9	10

Physical Environment Rating: Assessment:	1	2	3	4	5	6	7	8	9	10
Recreation/Rejuvenation Rating: Assessment:	1	2	3	4	5	6	7	8	9	10
Spiritual Rating: Assessment:	1	2	3	4	5	6	7	8	9	10
Personal Growth Rating: Assessment:	1	2	3	4	5	6	7	8	9	10

List here the three priority areas you want to work on with the highest priority listed as number one.

1. _____

2. _____

3. _____

How would each area have to change to improve its rating by two points? Here is an example: One of Marvin's three priority areas was Money Matters. Marvin gave his current Money Matters a score of 3 and wrote that he owed more than $5,000 on his credit cards and had only $200 in savings. In order to move his score from 3 to 5, Marvin decides he would have to pay off 30 percent of his credit card debt and double his savings.

Decide how your three priorities need to change to increase your rating two points:

1. _____

2. _____

3. _____

What is your number one priority? Write it here and create three SMART goals to help you achieve it.

For example, here are Marvin's SMART goals:

1. Stop using credit cards immediately and start paying cash.
2. Create and stick to a budget within thirty days from today.
3. Limit lunch and dinner out to once a month starting now.

Write your SMART goals here:

1. _____

2. _____

3. _____

CHECKLIST FOR SETTING BOUNDARIES

☐ Communicate.

☐ Learn to say no.

☐ Insist that you be treated fairly and with honesty.

☐ Require others to respect their commitments to you.

☐ Keep your top three priorities and their respective goals where you can see them and refer to them when you are unsure about committing your time to an activity.

☐ Be flexible and let yourself respond to the moment. Spontaneity can be healthy and creative.

☐ Other:

CHECKLIST FOR BECOMING A TIME-SAVVY TRAVELER

☐ Ask if this trip is necessary.

☐ Set goals for your trip.

☐ Create folders for meetings and locations.

☐ Create an itinerary that maximizes your time and minimizes your stress.

☐ Plan for delays and canceled flights.

☐ Find out what business amenities hotels offer.

☐ Join preferred flyer and hotel guest clubs.

☐ Book ground transportation.

☐ Obtain maps.

☐ Leave copies of your itinerary with your family and office.

☐ Create a Master List for ease of packing.

☐ Call the airline before leaving home to find out if your flight is on time.

☐ Check in according to the requirements of your airline.

☐ Double-check destination tags for checked luggage.

☐ Place a distinctive identification tag on your luggage.

☐ Bring something to occupy your time.

TRAVEL MASTER LIST

Outerwear	Undergarments
Toiletries	Equipment
Medical Kit	Supplies
Travel Documents	Sleepwear
Accessories	Business Documents and Materials
Reading Material	Other

CERTIFICATE OF ACHIEVEMENT

Instructor:

Title of program:

Date:

Location:

This certifies that _____ [name] has successfully completed the Time Management Workshop on _____ [date].

[Instructor's signature]

COURSE ASSESSMENT

Instructor:

Title of Program:

Date: Time:

Location:

For each item on the list, check the box that corresponds to the number that you believe applies to the item.

1 = Strongly disagree
2 = Disagree
3 = Not sure
4 = Agree
5 = Strongly agree

Item	1	2	3	4	5
I can apply the information from the workshop on my job.					
I can relate to the examples and problems in the workshop.					
I learned new skills to use on the job.					
I would recommend this workshop to other employees.					
Information was clearly communicated.					
Learning objectives for the workshop were clear.					
Learning objectives for the workshop were met.					
The handouts made it easier to apply the information to my job.					
The handouts were easy to use.					
The instructor was organized and efficient.					
The instructor encouraged participation.					
The instructor handled group discussions well.					
The instructor handled questions well.					
The instructor kept my interest.					

Item	1	2	3	4	5
The instructor knew the material.					
The instructor maintained control of the class.					
The instructor used examples I could relate to.					
The instructor used overheads effectively.					
The instructor was well prepared.					
The instructor's delivery was lively and interesting.					
The length of the workshop was about right.					
The modules were presented in a logical manner.					
The overheads added to the presentation.					
The overheads made it easier to understand the material.					
The pace of the workshop was appropriate.					
The individual exercises helped me apply the information to my job.					
The room was comfortable.					
The team activities were valuable.					
The workshop was fun.					

I believe that the workshop could be improved in the following way(s):

I liked these aspects of the workshop:

INDEX

NOTES

NOTES

NOTES

NOTES

NOTES

NOTES

NOTES

NOTES

NOTES

NOTES